M000238068

Series 65 Exam
Practice Question Workbook

Coventry House Publishing

Copyright © 2018 Coventry House Publishing

All rights reserved.

ISBN: 1732113750
ISBN-13: 978-1732113756

CONTENTS

PRACTICE EXAM 1

QUESTIONS

1. Which of the following is a notice made in the financial press that formally announces a particular transaction, such as an IPO or stock placement?

   A. Omitting prospectus
   B. Preliminary prospectus
   C. Red herring
   D. Tombstone ad

2. Which of the following is/are correct regarding stock splits and reverse stock splits?

   (1) A 3-for-1 stock split will decrease a stock's market price per share.
   (2) A reverse stock split is intended to increase a stock's market price per share.

   A. (1) only
   B. (2) only
   C. Both (1) and (2) are correct.
   D. Neither (1) or (2) are correct.

3. Which of the following is the minimum denomination of Treasury notes that can be purchased by an investor?

   A. $50
   B. $100
   C. $1,000
   D. $10,000

4. The statement of cash flows is separated into all but which of the following categories?

   A. Cash flow from financing activities
   B. Cash flow from income activities
   C. Cash flow from investing activities
   D. Cash flow from operating activities

5. Which of the following are permitted investments in an IRA?

   (1) Real estate
   (2) Money market funds
   (3) Common stock
   (4) Bond funds

   A. (3) and (4) only
   B. (1), (2), and (3) only
   C. (2), (3), and (4) only
   D. All of the above are correct.

6. Which of the following statements describes a typical whole life insurance policy?

(1) The premiums must be paid for the insured's entire lifetime, or for a period of at least ten years.
(2) The cash value cannot be used as collateral for a loan.
(3) The difference between a policy's face amount and the reserve must be greater than the cash surrender value at all times.
(4) The cash value must equal the face amount of coverage by the end of the mortality table.

A. (4) only
B. (2) and (3) only
C. (1), (2), and (3) only
D. All of the above are correct.

7. Which of the following is correct regarding a mutual fund's turnover rate?

A. The higher the turnover rate, the less tax efficient the mutual fund will be. Therefore, funds with high turnover rates are best positioned in taxable accounts.
B. The higher the turnover rate, the more tax efficient the mutual fund will be. Therefore, funds with low turnover rates are best positioned in tax-deferred accounts.
C. The higher the turnover rate, the less tax efficient the mutual fund will be. Therefore, funds with high turnover rates are best positioned in tax-deferred accounts.
D. None of the above are correct.

8. If an RIA has between _____ and _____ of assets under management, the RIA may register with either the applicable state(s) where the RIA maintains clients, or the SEC, at the RIA's discretion.

A. $10 million, $100 million
B. $25 million, $100 million
C. $50 million, $150 million
D. $100 million, $200 million

9. Which of the following are correct regarding the role of a trustee?

(1) A trustee is the legal owner of trust property.
(2) A trustee has a fiduciary duty to income beneficiaries only.
(3) A trustee must act at all times for the exclusive benefit of the beneficiaries or he or she may incur a legal liability.
(4) A trustee has a fiduciary duty to remainder beneficiaries only.

A. (1) and (3) only
B. (2) and (4) only
C. (1), (2), and (3) only
D. (1), (3), and (4) only

10. Which of the following is a system of taxation where one tax rate is applied to all personal income, with no deductions or offsets allowed?

A. Flat tax
B. General tax
C. Single payer tax
D. Value added tax

11. All but which of the following are correct regarding a bond's call provision?

A. It protects the issuer from declines in interest rates.
B. It will cause the investor's required rate of return to be lower.
C. It may be included in a bond agreement.
D. It allows the debtor to pay off the debt after a specific period of time at a predetermined price.

12. Defined benefit plans tend to favor older employees for which of the following reasons?

A. The future value of the participant's promised benefit is greater the less time remaining until retirement.
B. The present value of the participant's promised benefit is greater the less time remaining until retirement.
C. The future value of the participant's promised benefit is greater the more time remaining until retirement.
D. The present value of the participant's promised benefit is greater the more time remaining until retirement.

13. With certain exceptions, which of the following acts requires that firms or sole practitioners compensated for advising others about securities investments must register with the SEC and conform to regulations designed to protect investors?

A. Securities Act of 1933
B. Securities Exchange Act of 1934
C. Investment Advisers Act of 1940
D. Investment Company Act of 1940

14. An investor who believes that an economic recession is imminent should purchase which of the following type of stocks?

A. Defensive stocks because they tend to underperform during economic downturns.
B. Defensive stocks because they tend to outperform during economic downturns.
C. Cyclical stocks because they tend to outperform during economic downturns.
D. Cyclical stocks because they tend to underperform during economic downturns.

15. Assume that an investor's portfolio has a realized return of 16%. The realized return of the S&P 500 for the same time period is 18%, and the risk-free rate is 6%. If the beta of the portfolio is 0.75, what is the portfolio's alpha?

   A. –0.02
   B. –0.01
   C. +0.01
   D. +0.02

16. Which of the following accurately describes a complex trust?

   A. It's a trust with more than one beneficiary.
   B. It's a trust that may distribute income annually.
   C. It's a trust that reverts back to the grantor's estate at death.
   D. It's a trust that is required to distribute all of its income annually.

17. Which of the following is used to determine whether an instrument qualifies as an "investment contract" for the purposes of the Securities Act of 1933?

   A. The Howey test
   B. The Knight test
   C. The Lochner test
   D. The Ralston test

18. Kappa Inc., a growing IT company based in California, plans to launch its IPO this year. The IPO will be regulated by which of the following laws?

   A. Securities Act of 1933
   B. Securities Act of 1934
   C. Investment Company Act of 1940
   D. SIPC of 1970

19. Which of the following are characteristics of Series EE bonds?

   (1) They may be purchased for an amount equal to one-half of face value.
   (2) They may be purchased for a minimum price of $25 for a $50 bond.
   (3) The U.S. Treasury guarantees that an EE bond's value will double after 10 years.
   (4) They may be purchased for a maximum price of $5,000 for a $10,000 bond.

   A. (1) only
   B. (1), (2), and (4) only
   C. (2), (3), and (4) only
   D. All of the above are correct.

20. Which of the following is the illegal trading practice of manipulating the market by buying and selling a security to create the illusion of high trading activity and to attract other traders who may increase the price?

    A. Capping and pegging
    B. Front running
    C. Painting the tape
    D. Trading ahead

21. Earnings after taxes ÷ Common stockholder equity = _____

    A. Current ratio
    B. Net profit margin
    C. Operating profit margin
    D. Return on equity

22. Dr. Jones, age 29, recently opened a successful dental practice. She's concerned that her young employees will leave for a more experienced dental practice once they're fully trained. In order to retain her young employees, which retirement plan should Dr. Jones adopt?

    A. Cash balance plan
    B. Defined benefit plan
    C. Money purchase plan
    D. Target benefit plan

23. Which of the following mutual fund share classes will charge investors a front-end load?

    A. Class A shares
    B. Class B shares
    C. Class C shares
    D. Class D shares

24. All but which of the following are correct regarding "notice filing" by an RIA?

    A. Notice filing is required for an RIA to maintain its compliant registration status.
    B. While most jurisdictions will allow for a "de minimis" number of clients before requiring notice filing, some jurisdictions may require notice filing upon taking on the first client in that jurisdiction.
    C. Having a "place of business," as defined by applicable regulatory statutes, does not require notice filing unless the firm has 5 or more clients in the jurisdiction.
    D. All of the above are correct.

25. In order to be eligible to make a traditional IRA contribution, an individual must be younger than age _____ by the end of the taxable year.

   A. 59 ½
   B. 65
   C. 70 ½
   D. 71

26. Which of the following are backed by the full faith and credit of the government issuing the bonds and are repaid through taxes collected by the government body?

   A. General obligation bonds
   B. Moral obligation bonds
   C. Private purpose bonds
   D. Revenue bonds

27. Which of the following techniques can be used to reduce an individual's gross estate, and therefore, reduce estate taxes?

   A. Family limited partnership
   B. Payable on death account
   C. Living trust
   D. Totten trust

28. Which of the following regulations governs the extension of credit by broker-dealers and controls the margin requirements for stock purchases?

   A. Regulation D
   B. Regulation S
   C. Regulation T
   D. Regulation U

The following information relates to questions 29 – 31.

Alex had several capital gains and losses for the current year. His long-term capital gains were $3,200, his long-term capital losses were $2,800, his short-term capital gains were $800, and his short-term capital losses were $3,500.

29. What is the amount of net long-term capital gains?

   A. $0
   B. $400
   C. $700
   D. $2,400

30. What is the amount of net short-term capital gains?

   A. –$2,700
   B. –$700
   C. –$400
   D. $0

31. What is the total calculated capital gain or capital loss?

   A. $2,300 net short-term capital loss
   B. $2,300 net short-term capital gain
   C. $3,000 net short-term capital loss
   D. $3,000 net short-term capital gain

32. Which of the following is a characteristic of a variable life insurance policy?

   A. Premiums and death benefits are flexible.
   B. A minimum death benefit is guaranteed.
   C. It is made up of increasing units of term insurance and a guaranteed cash value.
   D. The death benefit is linked to the performance of the S&P 500 only.

33. Which of the following rules establishes standards for the content, approval, record-keeping, and filing of communications with FINRA, and must be followed by firms when communicating with the public, including communications with retail and institutional investors?

   A. FINRA Rule 2111
   B. FINRA Rule 2210
   C. FINRA Rule 3240
   D. FINRA Rule 3270

34. Assume the next dividend for Epsilon stock will be $3 per share, and investors require a 12% rate of return to purchase the stock. If the dividend for Epsilon stock increases by 4% each year, what price should the stock be selling for today?

   A. $22.50 per share
   B. $27.50 per share
   C. $32.50 per share
   D. $37.50 per share

35. An option that can be exercised only at its expiration date is a/an _____ style option.

   A. American
   B. Asian
   C. Australian
   D. European

36. Which of the following is the oldest international investor protection organization and is an association of state securities administrators who are charged with the responsibility to protect consumers who purchase securities or investment advice? Its membership consists of administrators from the territories, districts, and states of the U.S., Mexico, and Canada.

    A. NAIC
    B. NASAA
    C. NASD
    D. NSCC

37. In which of the following does the donor transfer income-producing property to a reversionary trust, and then directs the trust income to be transferred to a qualified charity initially for a period of time not to exceed twenty years?

    A. Charitable lead trust
    B. Charitable remainder trust
    C. Grantor retained trust
    D. Pooled income fund

38. All but which of the following are correct regarding the Securities Exchange Act of 1934?

    A. It created the SEC.
    B. It regulates securities transactions in the secondary market.
    C. It is referred to as the "truth in securities" law.
    D. It includes provisions for other areas of securities law, including insider trading, antifraud, and proxy solicitation.

39. All but which of the following are correct regarding a "not held" order?

    A. It applies mainly to international equities.
    B. It is a market or limit order in which the customer does not want to transact automatically at the inside market, but instead has given the broker time and price discretion in transacting on a best-efforts basis.
    C. The customer is placing full confidence in the broker to execute the trade at the best price.
    D. The broker may be held liable for missing the price within the limits (limit not held) or obtaining a worse price (market not held).

40. On a company's balance sheet, assets are reported at their:

    A. discounted value.
    B. expected future value.
    C. fair market value.
    D. original cost.

For questions 41 – 45, match the type of retirement plan with the description that follows. Use only one answer per blank. Answers may be used more than once or not at all.

A. Money purchase plan
B. Target benefit plan
C. Flat benefit plan
D. SEP
E. Cash balance plan
F. Profit sharing plan
G. Unit benefit plan

41. ___ A plan similar to a defined benefit plan because contributions are based on projected retirement benefits.

42. ___ A type of defined contribution plan that is not a pension plan.

43. ___ A defined benefit plan that defines the employee's benefit in terms that are more characteristic of a defined contribution plan.

44. ___ The employer calculates the contribution by multiplying an employee's years of service by a percentage of his or her salary.

45. ___ A plan that requires a fixed percentage of compensation be contributed for each eligible employee.

46. Which of the following is a fraudulent investment operation where the operator provides fabricated reports and generates investment returns for older investors through revenue paid by new investors, rather than from legitimate business activities or profits of financial trading?

A. Pump and dump scheme
B. Ponzi scheme
C. Matrix scheme
D. Bucket shop scheme

47. Erin inherited shares of Beta stock that are currently valued at $850,000. To retire and maintain her lifestyle, she requires a fixed 6% payout for life. Which of the following trusts will allow Erin to achieve her goal?

A. Charitable remainder annuity trust
B. Charitable remainder unitrust
C. Charitable lead annuity trust
D. Charitable lead unitrust

48. An investment adviser will be deemed to have custody of client assets if which of the following apply?

    A. The advisor has possession of client funds or securities and does not return them to the client within 3 days.
    B. The advisor is authorized or permitted to withdraw client funds or securities.
    C. The adviser has legal ownership or access to client funds or securities.
    D. All of the above are correct.

49. All but which of the following are characteristics of American Depository Receipts (ADRs)?

    A. They are traded on secondary exchanges.
    B. They represent ownership interest in foreign securities denominated in U.S. dollars.
    C. They involve banks collecting money in U.S. dollars and then converting into foreign currency for ADR holders.
    D. They are issued by banks in foreign countries.

50. Which of the following was adopted to update short sale regulations and to address concerns regarding potentially abusive naked short selling?

    A. Regulation BTR
    B. Regulation HFT
    C. Regulation NMS
    D. Regulation SHO

51. In 2016, Theta LLC reported total revenue of $800,000, total expenses of $650,000, and net income of $150,000. If accounts receivable increased by $90,000, then how much cash did Theta LLC receive from customers?

    A. $560,000
    B. $710,000
    C. $800,000
    D. $890,000

52. All but which of the following are correct regarding the Central Registration Depository (CRD)?

    A. It was developed by NASAA and the NASD.
    B. It consolidated a multiple paper-based state licensing and regulatory process into a single, nationwide computer system.
    C. Its computerized database contains the licensing and disciplinary histories on more than 650,000 securities professionals and 5,200 securities firms.
    D. All of the above are correct.

53. The Russell 2000 measures the performance of _____ U.S. stocks.

    A. small-cap
    B. mid-cap
    C. large-cap
    D. blended

54. Which of the following is correct regarding commercial paper?

    A. It has a maturity of 270 days or less.
    B. It's issued in denominations of $1,000 or more.
    C. It does not act as a viable substitute for short-term bank financing.
    D. It has less default risk than Treasury bills.

55. Which of the following is considered a hybrid security?

    A. Common stock
    B. Corporate bond
    C. Preferred stock
    D. REIT

For questions 56 – 62, match the economic indicator with the description that follows. Use only one answer per blank. Answers may be used more than once or not at all.

    A. Leading economic indicator
    B. Lagging economic indicator

56. ___ Change in consumer sentiment

57. ___ Average prime rate charged by banks

58. ___ Change in the Consumer Price Index (CPI)

59. ___ Orders for durable goods

60. ___ Average duration of unemployment

61. ___ Change in money supply

62. ___ Housing starts

63. Which of the following is correct regarding Coverdell Education Savings Accounts (ESAs)?

   A. Private elementary school expenses are permitted to be paid from an ESA.
   B. The maximum annual contribution to an ESA is $5,000.
   C. Secondary school expenses are not permitted to be paid from an ESA.
   D. All of the above are correct.

64. Which of the following investment strategies is profitable in a declining stock market?

   (1) Buying a call
   (2) Buying a put
   (3) Selling a put
   (4) Selling a call

   A. (1) and (3) only
   B. (1) and (4) only
   C. (2) and (3) only
   D. (2) and (4) only

65. Which of the following will result if a distribution is taken from a health savings account (HSA) by an individual under age 65, and the distribution is not used to pay for qualified medical expenses?

   A. The distribution is subject to ordinary income tax only.
   B. The distribution is subject to ordinary income tax and a 10% penalty.
   C. The distribution is subject to ordinary income tax and a 15% penalty.
   D. The distribution is not subject to tax.

66. An IRA must be created and funded by _____ of the calendar year following the year in which the contribution applies.

   A. January 1
   B. April 15
   C. June 31
   D. December 31

67. Which of the following theories is based on the assumption that investors are risk averse, and they will prefer higher returns to lower returns for a given level of risk?

   A. Arbitrage pricing theory
   B. Black-scholes valuation theory
   C. Efficient market theory
   D. Modern portfolio theory

68. What is the taxable equivalent yield of a municipal bond that has a tax-free yield of 6%? Assume the investor is in the 28% tax bracket.

A. 4.69%
B. 7.68%
C. 8.33%
D. 21.43%

69. All but which of the following are correct regarding the tenancy by entirety form of property ownership?

A. It is an interest in property that can be held only by spouses.
B. The property automatically passes to the surviving spouse when one spouse dies.
C. It is an interest in property that can be held by non-spouses in an incorporated business such as an LLC, S Corp, or C Corp.
D. In most states, it is not severable by an individual spouse.

70. Which of the following are characteristics of a zero-coupon bond?

(1) It does not make periodic interest payments throughout the term of the bond.
(2) It has significant reinvestment risk because no payments are made until the bond matures.
(3) It requires taxes to be paid on accrued interest each year, even though no interest is received.
(4) The duration of a zero-coupon bond is less than its term to maturity.

A. (1) and (3) only
B. (2) and (4) only
C. (1), (2), and (3) only
D. (2), (3), and (4) only

71. All but which of the following are characteristics of exchange-traded funds (ETFs)?

A. They are traded on an exchange like individual securities.
B. Their trades settle at the end of the trading day, similar to mutual funds.
C. They have lower expenses than mutual funds.
D. They are income tax efficient.

72. According to FINRA Rule 3240, which of the following is correct regarding borrowing and lending arrangements between an RIA and its customers?

A. The specific borrowing/lending arrangement must meet certain conditions, such as the customer cannot be an immediate family member.
B. Proper notification of the borrowing or lending arrangement must be given, but advanced approval is not required.
C. The member firm must have a written policy in place regarding borrowing and lending arrangements.
D. All of the above are correct.

73. A stock with a beta of −1.5 and a standard deviation of 10.1 will change in which of the following ways if the stock market increases 8%?

A. Increase by 4%
B. Increase by 8%
C. Decrease by 10%
D. Decrease by 12%

74. _____ risk cannot be eliminated through diversification because it affects the entire market. _____ risk may be diversified away or avoided by not investing in securities that exhibit the risk.

A. Non-systematic, Unsystematic
B. Unsystematic, Systematic
C. Systematic, Unsystematic
D. Total, Systematic

75. Short-term capital gains tax rates apply if an asset is held for:

A. 12 months or less.
B. less than 12 months.
C. 6 months or less using the half-year convention.
D. less than 6 months using the half-year convention.

76. The Bank Secrecy Act of 1970 requires financial institutions to assist U.S. government agencies in detecting and preventing money laundering by filing reports of cash transactions exceeding which of the following daily aggregate amounts?

A. $5,000
B. $10,000
C. $50,000
D. $100,000

77. Your client is interested in participating in his company's qualified retirement plan. He has completed one year of service and assumed that he was now eligible to participate. However, his employer will not let him enroll in the plan until next year. You tell your client that eligibility may be postponed until the completion of his second year of service if which of the following conditions apply?

A. The employer agrees to match 100% of employee deferrals up to 10% of compensation.
B. Contributions are made based on an age-weighted formula.
C. Contributions are 100% immediately vested upon eligibility.
D. Key employees must wait three years to enroll.

78. Which of the following rules permits the public resale of restricted or control securities if a number of conditions are met, including how long the securities are held, the way in which they are sold, and the amount that can be sold at any one time?

    A. Securities Act Rule 144
    B. Securities Act Rule 405
    C. Securities Act Rule 433
    D. Securities Act Rule 506

79. Which of the following variables are used to calculate a stock's beta coefficient?

    (1) The standard deviation of the return for a particular security.
    (2) The correlation coefficient between the return for a particular security and the return for the overall market.
    (3) The standard deviation of the return for the overall market.
    (4) The coefficient of determination.

    A. (2) only
    B. (4) only
    C. (1) and (3) only
    D. (1), (2), and (3) only

The following information relates to questions 80 – 81.

Earlier this year, Pete exchanged a $500,000 ordinary life insurance policy for an annuity. He paid $90,000 in premiums over the life of the policy, and the cash value at the time of the exchange was $62,000.

80. What is Pete's basis in the annuity?

    A. $28,000
    B. $62,000
    C. $90,000
    D. $152,000

81. What would be Pete's basis if he used $25,000 of dividends to reduce the premium?

    A. $62,000
    B. $65,000
    C. $90,000
    D. $115,000

82. Which of the following corporate voting procedures entitles a shareholder to one vote per share, and votes must be divided evenly among the candidates being voted on?

    A. Accumulated voting
    B. Cumulative voting
    C. Non-regulatory voting
    D. Statutory voting

83. A participant in a defined contribution plan is least affected by which of the following factors?

A. Account balance
B. Investment performance
C. Life expectancy
D. Pre-retirement inflation

84. Which of the following is/are correct regarding the capital structure of closed-end mutual funds?

(1) A closed-end mutual fund has a fixed number of shares that, after original issue, trade on the secondary market.
(2) The price an investor pays when buying shares of a closed-end mutual fund is based on supply and demand.

A. (1) only
B. (2) only
C. Both (1) and (2) are correct.
D. Neither (1) or (2) are correct.

85. Which of the following is the measure of a company's ability to pay its debt obligations?

A. Return on debt
B. Return on assets
C. Times interest earned ratio
D. Turnover ratio

For questions 86 – 88, match the dividend date with the description that follows. Use only one answer per blank. Answers may be used more than once or not at all.

A. Date of declaration
B. Ex-dividend date
C. Date of record
D. Date of payment

86. ___ The date that the board of directors approves and decides that a dividend will be paid.

87. ___ The date that it is determined who owns stock in the company and is entitled to receive a dividend.

88. ___ The date that the market price of the stock adjusts for the dividend.

89. Which of the following option strategies involves an investor holding a position in both a call and put for the same underlying security, with the same strike price and expiration date?

A. Collar
B. Naked call
C. Spread
D. Straddle

90. In 2017, the SEC adopted an amendment to the Settlement Cycle Rule under the Securities Exchange Act of 1934 that changed the standard settlement cycle for most broker-dealer transactions in which of the following ways?

A. The standard settlement cycle was shortened from 3 business days after the trade (T+3) to 2 business days after the trade (T+2).
B. The standard settlement cycle was shortened from 2 business days after the trade (T+2) to 1 business day after the trade (T+1).
C. The standard settlement cycle was lengthened from 1 business day after the trade (T+1) to 2 business days after the trade (T+2).
D. The standard settlement cycle was lengthened from 2 business days after the trade (T+2) to 3 business days after the trade (T+3).

91. A federal gift tax return must be filed if which of the following events occur?

A. A gift of a future interest in property has been made for $5,000.
B. Spouses have split a $5,000 gift of individually owned property.
C. The gifts from a donor to any single donee for a calendar year exceed the amount of the gift tax annual exclusion.
D. All of the above are correct.

92. SEC-registered investment advisers must deliver which of the following to each client or prospective client?

A. Form ADV Part 2A (brochure) only
B. Form ADV Part 2 (brochure supplement) only
C. Form ADV Part 2A (brochure) and Part 2 (brochure supplement)
D. Form ADV Part 1 and Part 2A (brochure)

93. Which of the following are profitability ratios?

(1) Operating profit margin
(2) Net profit margin
(3) Return on assets
(4) Return on equity

A. (3) and (4) only
B. (1), (2), and (3) only
C. (1), (3), and (4) only
D. All of the above are correct.

94. Kappa Inc., a C Corp, had a profitable year and has extra money to invest. The owners would like to maximize the after-tax income to the corporation. Which of the following investments would best help them achieve their goal?

A. Value stocks
B. Preferred stock
C. Municipal bonds
D. Highly-rated corporate bonds

95. Which of the following occurs when the supply of goods and services exceeds their demand?

A. Deflation
B. Inflation
C. Stagflation
D. Price stability

96. Which of the following is the formula to calculate an investment's public offering price (POP)?

A. POP = NAV ÷ Sales charge
B. POP = Sales charge ÷ NAV
C. POP = NAV + Sales charge
D. POP = NAV – Sales charge

97. Which of the following is a self-liquidating investment in real estate mortgages and mortgage-backed securities?

A. GIC
B. REIT
C. REMIC
D. UIT

98. Which of the following is the FINRA-developed vehicle that facilitates the mandatory reporting of over-the-counter secondary market transactions in eligible fixed income securities? All broker-dealers who are FINRA member firms have an obligation to report transactions in corporate bonds to this vehicle under an SEC-approved set of rules.

A. ACT
B. AML
C. CTR
D. TRACE

99. Which of the following is the market value of all the goods and services produced in one year by labor and property supplied by the citizens of a country, wherever they are located?

A. GDP
B. GNP
C. NDP
D. NNP

100. According to Regulation D, firms may sell private placements to how many non-accredited investors in a 12-month period?

A. 0
B. 25
C. 35
D. 50

101. Which of the following are permitted distribution options from a qualified retirement plan?

(1) Lump sum distribution
(2) Direct trustee-to-trustee transfer
(3) Payment in the form of an annuity or other periodic payment option
(4) Rollover of funds from one qualified retirement plan to another

A. (1) and (3) only
B. (1), (2), and (4) only
C. (2), (3), and (4) only
D. All of the above are correct.

102. A call is an option to _____ a specified number of shares of stock during a specified period at a specified price. A buyer of a call option expects the price of the underlying stock to _____.

A. buy, fall
B. buy, rise
C. sell, fall
D. sell, rise

103. All but which of the following are underlying assumptions of the capital asset pricing model (CAPM)?

A. All investors have the same one-period time horizon.
B. All investors have the same expectations about the risk-return relationship of assets.
C. Investors can borrow and lend at a specific risk-free rate of return equal to zero.
D. There are no transaction costs, taxes, or inflation.

104. According to FINRA's eligibility requirements, statutory disqualification will result for certain misdemeanors and all felony criminal convictions for a period of _____ from the date of conviction.

   A. 5 years
   B. 10 years
   C. 15 years
   D. 20 years

105. Which of the following is a set of documents, including a prospectus, which a company must file with the SEC pursuant to the Securities Act of 1933 before it proceeds with a public offering?

   A. Prospectus statement
   B. Red herring
   C. Registration statement
   D. Tombstone ad

106. According to the principles of behavioral finance, which theory suggests that investors typically fear losses more than they value gains? As a result, investors will often choose the smaller of two potential gains if it avoids a highly probable loss.

   A. Game theory
   B. Prospect theory
   C. Utility theory
   D. Zero sum theory

107. If interest rates _____ following a bond issue, a sinking-fund provision will allow the issuing company to reduce the interest rate risk of its bonds as it replaces a portion of the existing debt with _____ bonds.

   A. decline, higher yielding
   B. decline, lower yielding
   C. rise, higher yielding
   D. rise, lower yielding

108. Which of the following is a daily publication of the National Quotation Bureau that details the bid and asked prices of corporate bonds traded in the over-the-counter market?

   A. Blue sheets
   B. Pink sheets
   C. White sheets
   D. Yellow sheets

109. The efficient market hypothesis suggests all but which of the following?

   A. Investors are unable to outperform the stock market on a consistent basis.
   B. Daily fluctuations in stock prices are a result of modern portfolio theory.
   C. The stock market's efficiency in valuing securities is rapid and accurate.
   D. Any excess returns are temporary and will regress to the mean.

110. Gamma Inc. provides the following information for the fiscal year:

Net income	$660,000
Number of shares outstanding	40,000
Price per share	$19.50
Total assets	$3,250,000
Total liabilities	$2,980,000

   What is Gamma Inc.'s book value?

   A. $78,000
   B. $192,000
   C. $270,000
   D. $930,000

111. All but which of the following are correct regarding pooled income funds?

   A. A pooled income fund is generally created by a public charity, such as a private or public higher education institution or a not-for-profit hospital.
   B. A benefit of a pooled income fund is that it can invest in tax-exempt securities.
   C. In a pooled income fund, the donor's gifted property is commingled with property transferred by other donors.
   D. Additional contributions of property are permitted into a pooled income fund.

112. Which of the following are among the goals of the Federal Reserve?

   A. To achieve full employment.
   B. To minimize systematic risk.
   C. To stabilize prices.
   D. All of the above are correct.

113. Which of the following is a tax imposed in such a manner that the tax rate decreases as the amount subject to taxation increases?

   A. Corporate tax
   B. Progressive tax
   C. Regressive tax
   D. Value added tax

114. Which of the following has the mission of protecting investors, municipal entities, and the public interest by promoting a fair and efficient municipal market, regulating firms that engage in municipal securities and advisory activities, and promoting market transparency?

    A. AMBAC
    B. FNMA
    C. GNMA
    D. MSRB

115. A large interest rate change has the most significant effect on a _____ bond.

    A. low coupon
    B. short duration
    C. high coupon
    D. short maturity

116. Which of the following lists the assets provided in the correct order from most liquid to least liquid?

    (1) Real estate
    (2) Treasury bills
    (3) Limited partnership
    (4) Investment-grade corporate bonds

    A. 2, 1, 4, 3
    B. 4, 2, 3, 1
    C. 3, 1, 4, 2
    D. 2, 4, 1, 3

117. Which of the following is/are correct regarding the objectives of ERISA?

    (1) ERISA requires retirement plan sponsors to disclose full and accurate information about qualified retirement plan activity to all participants.
    (2) ERISA guarantees future benefits at a minimum level for defined benefit plans as part of the PBGC.

    A. (1) only
    B. (2) only
    C. Both (1) and (2) are correct.
    D. Neither (1) or (2) are correct.

118. Treasury STRIPS are always issued at a:

    A. premium to par.
    B. discount to par.
    C. price equal to par.
    D. price above or equal to par.

119. Lauren purchased a bond with a face value of $1,000 and a coupon rate of 4.5%. Her effective tax rate is 25%. If the risk-free rate is 4%, and coupon payments are made semiannually, what is the periodic interest payment?

    A. $16.88, paid twice per year.
    B. $22.50, paid twice per year.
    C. $45.00, paid once per year.
    D. $45.00, paid twice per year.

120. In addition to the federal securities laws, each state has its own set of securities laws, commonly referred to as _____, which are designed to protect investors against fraudulent sales practices and activities.

    A. Blue ocean laws
    B. Blue sky laws
    C. Green field laws
    D. Open field laws

121. Which of the following is correct regarding TIPS?

    A. Investors are paid either the adjusted principal amount at maturity, or the original principal amount, whichever is greater.
    B. They pay interest annually.
    C. The payments increase with inflation but never decrease.
    D. They have a final maturity up to 10 years from the date of issue.

122. Which of the following is a contract between an investor and an issuer in which the issuer guarantees payment of a stated sum to the investor at some set date in the future? In return for this future payment, the investor agrees to pay the issuer a set amount of money either as a lump sum or in periodic installments.

    A. ETN
    B. FAC
    C. ISO
    D. NQSO

123. Which of the following is a theory stating that an investment company that passes all capital gains, interest, and dividends through to its shareholders shouldn't be taxed at the corporate level?

    A. Capital gain theory
    B. Conduit theory
    C. Passive income theory
    D. Tax harvest theory

124. Which of the following is an order to purchase a security at or below a specified price?

A. Buy stop order
B. Buy market order
C. Buy limit order
D. None of the above are correct.

125. All but which of the following are correct regarding advertising activities engaged in by an RIA?

A. Advertisements include any notice, circular, or letter addressed to more than one person.
B. Social media communications, such as Twitter feeds and online blogs, are not considered advertisements.
C. Advertisement are not permitted to use the initials "RIA" or "IAR."
D. All of the above are correct.

126. The FDIC maintains stability and public confidence in the nation's financial system by doing all but which of the following?

A. Insuring deposits.
B. Managing receiverships.
C. Examining and supervising financial institutions for safety, soundness, and consumer protection.
D. Setting minimum standards for voluntarily established pension and health plans.

127. Which of the following acts was intended to reshape the U.S. regulatory system in a number of areas including consumer protection, trading restrictions, credit ratings, regulation of financial products, corporate governance and disclosure, and transparency?

A. Patriot Act of 2001
B. Sarbanes-Oxley Act of 2002
C. Fair and Accurate Credit Transactions Act of 2003
D. Dodd-Frank Wall Street Reform and Consumer Protection Act of 2010

128. Which of the following is/are correct regarding a bond's coupon rate?

(1) The smaller a bond's coupon, the greater its relative price fluctuation.
(2) The smaller a bond's coupon, the greater its reinvestment risk.

A. (1) only
B. (2) only
C. Both (1) and (2) are correct.
D. Neither (1) or (2) are correct.

129. Which of the following insures the interest and principal payments for municipal bonds and other public finance debt obligations?

    A. AMBAC
    B. DOL
    C. FDIC
    D. PBGC

130. All but which of the following are types of annuity settlement options?

    A. Extended term
    B. Installment refund
    C. Life with period certain
    D. Single life

ANSWER KEY

1. D
A tombstone ad is a notice made in the financial press that formally announces a particular transaction, such as an IPO or stock placement.

2. C
A 3-for-1 stock split will decrease a stock's market price per share. A reverse stock split is intended to increase a stock's market price per share.

3. B
Treasury notes are sold in minimum denominations of $100.

4. A
The statement of cash flows in separated into the following three categories: cash flow from income activities, cash flow from investing activities, and cash flow from operating activities.

5. D
IRAs may invest in all four types of investments, including real estate (REITs).

6. A
The cash value of a whole life insurance policy must equal the face amount of coverage by the end of the mortality table.

7. C
The higher the turnover rate, the less tax efficient the mutual fund will be. Therefore, funds with high turnover rates are best positioned in tax-deferred accounts.

8. B
If an RIA has between $25 million and $100 million of assets under management, the RIA may register with either the applicable state(s) where the RIA maintains clients, or the SEC. Due to legislation, exceptions may apply.

9. A
A trustee is the legal owner of trust property. A trustee must act at all times for the exclusive benefit of the beneficiaries or he or she may incur a legal liability. A trustee has a fiduciary duty to all trust beneficiaries regardless of whether they are income or remainder beneficiaries.

10. A
A flat tax is a system of taxation where one tax rate is applied to all personal income, with no deductions or offsets allowed.

11. B
A bond's call provision may be included in a bond agreement, and it allows the debtor to pay off the debt after a specific period of time at a predetermined price. It protects the issuer from declines in interest rates. If a bond is callable it will cause an investor's required rate of return to be higher.

12. B
Defined benefit plans tend to favor older employees because the present value of the participant's promised benefit is greater the less time remaining until retirement.

13. C
With certain exceptions, the Investment Advisers Act of 1940 requires that firms or sole practitioners compensated for advising others about securities investments must register with the SEC and conform to regulations designed to protect investors.

14. B
An investor who believes that an economic recession is imminent should purchase defensive stocks because they tend to outperform during economic downturns.

15. C
$$\alpha_p = R_p - [R_f + \beta_p(R_m - R_f)]$$
$$\alpha_p = 0.16 - [0.06 + 0.75(0.18 - 0.06)] = 0.01$$

16. B
In a complex trust, income may be distributed, but it is not required. The trustee has the discretion to accumulate income. Unlike a complex trust, a simple trust must distribute all of its income annually.

17. A
The Howey test is the result of the U.S. Supreme Court case, Securities and Exchange Commission v. W. J. Howey Co. from 1946. It is used to determine whether an instrument qualifies as an "investment contract" for the purposes of the Securities Act of 1933.

18. A
The Securities Act of 1933 regulates new securities, including IPOs.

19. B
Series EE bonds may be purchased for an amount equal to one-half of face value. The minimum price is $25 for a $50 bond, and the maximum price is $5,000 for a $10,000 bond. At a minimum, the U.S. Treasury guarantees that an EE bond's value will double after 20 years.

20. C
Painting the tape is the illegal trading practice of manipulating the market by buying and selling a security to create the illusion of high trading activity and to attract other traders who may increase the price.

21. D
Earnings after taxes ÷ Common stockholder equity = Return on equity

22. C
The cash balance plan, defined benefit plan, and target benefit plan all favor older employees. Money purchase plans guarantee a contribution will be made each year and will help Dr. Jones achieve her goal of retaining her young employees.

23. A
Class A mutual fund shares charge a front-end load.

24. C
Notice filing is required for an RIA to maintain its compliant registration status. While most jurisdictions will allow for a "de minimis" number of clients before requiring notice filing, some jurisdictions may require notice filing upon taking on the first client in that jurisdiction. Having a "place of business," as defined by applicable regulatory statutes, in a state will require notice filing regardless of the number of clients in that jurisdiction.

25. C
In order to be eligible to make a traditional IRA contribution, an individual must be younger than age 70 ½ by the end of the taxable year.

26. A
General obligation bonds are backed by the full faith and credit of the government issuing the bonds and are repaid through taxes collected by the government body.

27. A
A family limited partnership can be used to reduce an individual's gross estate, and therefore, reduce estate taxes. The other items may be used to reduce an individual's probate estate, but not his or her gross estate.

28. C
Regulation T governs the extension of credit by broker-dealers and controls the margin requirements for stock purchases.

29. B
$3,200 – $2,800 = $400 net long-term capital gain

30. A
$3,500 – $800 = $2,700 net short-term capital loss

31. A
$2,700 – $400 = $2,300 net short-term capital loss

32. B
Variable life insurance policies have fixed premiums and provide a guaranteed minimum death benefit. The cash value is linked to the performance of underlying investments, which may include the S&P 500.

33. B
FINRA Rule 2210 establishes standards for the content, approval, recordkeeping, and filing of communications with FINRA, and must be followed by firms when communicating with the public, including communications with retail and institutional investors.

34. D
Price $= D_1 \div (r - g)$
Price $= \$3 \div (0.12 - 0.04) = \$37.50$ per share

35. D
An option that can be exercised only at its expiration date is a European style option.

36. B
The NASAA (North American Securities Administrators Association) is the oldest international investor protection organization and is an association of state securities administrators who are charged with the responsibility to protect consumers who purchase securities or investment advice. Its membership consists of administrators from the territories, districts, and states of the U.S., Mexico, and Canada.

37. A
In a charitable lead trust, the donor transfers income-producing property to a reversionary trust, and then directs the trust income to be transferred to a qualified charity initially for a period of time not to exceed twenty years.

38. C
The Securities Exchange Act of 1934 created the SEC, regulates the securities transactions in the secondary market, and includes provisions for other areas of securities law, including insider trading, antifraud, and proxy solicitation. The "truth in securities" law is another name for the Securities Act of 1933.

39. D
With a "not held" order, the broker will not be held responsible for missing the price within the limits (limit not held) or obtaining a worse price (market not held). A "not held" order applies mainly to international equities, and it's a market or limit order in which the customer does not want to transact automatically at the inside market, but instead has given the broker time and price discretion in transacting on a best-efforts basis. The customer is placing full confidence in the broker to execute the trade at the best price.

40. C
On a company's balance sheet, assets are reported at their fair market value.

41. B
A target benefit plan is similar to a defined benefit plan because contributions are based on projected retirement benefits.

42. F
Defined contribution plans can be either pension plans or profit sharing plans.

43. E
A cash balance plan is a type of defined benefit plan that defines the employee's benefit in terms that are more characteristic of a defined contribution plan.

44. G
In a unit benefit plan, the employer calculates the contribution by multiplying an employee's years of service by a percentage of his or her salary.

45. A
A money purchase plan requires that a fixed percentage of compensation be contributed for each eligible employee.

46. B
A Ponzi scheme is a fraudulent investment operation where the operator provides fabricated reports and generates returns for older investors through revenue paid by new investors, rather than from legitimate business activities or profits of financial trading.

47. A
A charitable remainder annuity trust (CRAT) can pay Erin a fixed percentage of the initial fair market value of the trust. With a charitable remainder unitrust (CRUT), the annual payout would be based on the fair market value of the trust revalued annually.

48. D
An investment advisor will be deemed to have custody of client assets if the advisor has possession of client funds or securities and does not return them to the client within 3 days, the advisor is authorized or permitted to withdraw client funds or securities, or the adviser has legal ownership or access to client funds or securities.

49. C
For ADRs, banks collect money in their local currency and then convert to U.S. dollars. ADRs are traded on secondary exchanges and represent ownership interest in foreign securities denominated in U.S. dollars. They are issued by banks in foreign countries.

50. D
Regulation SHO was adopted to update short sale regulations and to address concerns regarding potentially abusive naked short selling.

51. B
Cash received from customers = Revenue – Increase in accounts receivable
Cash received from customers = $800,000 – $90,000 = $710,000

52. D
The Central Registration Depository (CRD) was developed by NASAA and the NASD, and it consolidated a multiple paper-based state licensing and regulatory process into a single, nationwide computer system. Its computerized database contains the licensing and disciplinary histories on more than 650,000 securities professionals and 5,200 securities firms.

53. A
The Russell 2000 measures the performance of small-cap U.S. stocks.

54. A
Commercial paper has a maturity of 270 days or less and is issued in denominations of $100,000 or more.

55. C
Preferred stock is considered a hybrid security because it has characteristics of both common stock and fixed-income investments.

56. A
A change in consumer sentiment is a leading economic indicator.

57. B
The average prime rate charged by banks is a lagging economic indicator.

58. B
A change in the Consumer Price Index (CPI) is a lagging economic indicator.

59. A
Orders for durable goods are a leading economic indicator.

60. B
The average duration of unemployment is a lagging economic indicator.

61. A
A change in the money supply is a leading economic indicator.

62. A
Housing starts are a leading economic indicator.

63. A
Money in a Coverdell Education Savings Account (ESA) may be used to pay private elementary and/or secondary school expenses. The maximum contribution to an ESA is $2,000 per beneficiary per year.

64. D
Buying a put and selling a call are bearish strategies that are profitable in a declining stock market.

65. B
Distributions from a health savings account (HSA) that are not used to pay for qualified medical expenses are subject to ordinary income tax and a 10% penalty. The penalty is waived if the individual is age 65 or older.

66. B
An IRA must be created and funded by April 15 of the calendar year following the year in which the contribution applies.

67. D
Modern portfolio theory is based on the assumption that investors are risk averse, and they will prefer higher returns to lower returns for a given level of risk.

68. C
Taxable equivalent yield $= 0.06 \div (1 - 0.28) = 0.0833 = 8.33\%$

69. C
Tenancy by entirety is a form of joint tenancy allowed only for married couples. The property automatically passes to the surviving spouse when one spouse dies, and in most states it is not severable by an individual spouse.

70. A
A zero-coupon bond does not make periodic interest payments, however it requires taxes to be paid on accrued interest each year. A zero-coupon bond has no reinvestment risk, and its duration is equal to its term to maturity.

71. B
Exchange-traded funds (ETFs) may be bought or sold throughout the trading day like individual securities. They have lower expenses than mutual funds and are income tax efficient.

72. C
According to FINRA Rule 3240, borrowing and lending arrangements between an RIA and its customers requires the member firm to have a written policy in place.

73. D
$8\% \times -1.5 = -12\%$
A stock with a beta of −1.5 will move 150% in the opposite direction of the market. Therefore, if the stock market increases by 8%, the stock will decrease by 12%.

74. C
Systematic risk cannot be eliminated through diversification because it affects the entire market. Unsystematic risk may be diversified away or avoided by not investing in securities that exhibit the risk.

75. A
Short-term capital gains tax rates apply if an asset is held for 12 months or less.

76. B
The Bank Secrecy Act of 1970 requires financial institutions to assist U.S. government agencies in detecting and preventing money laundering by filing reports of cash transactions exceeding $10,000 (daily aggregate amount).

77. C
An employer can make an employee wait until he or she has completed the second year of service before enrolling in a qualified retirement plan. However, the employee must become 100% immediately vested in all future contributions allocated to his or her account.

78. A
Securities Act Rule 144 permits the public resale of restricted or control securities if a number of conditions are met, including how long the securities are held, the way in which they are sold, and the amount that can be sold at any one time.

79. D
The beta coefficient is calculated by dividing the standard deviation of the return for a particular security by the standard deviation of the return for the overall market, and then multiplying the result by the correlation coefficient of the two returns.

80. C
Pete's basis in the annuity is $90,000, which represents his premium payments in the life insurance policy.

81. B
$90,000 – $25,000 = $65,000
Pete's basis would have been equal to the premium payments ($90,000) less the dividends used to reduce the premium ($25,000).

82. D
Statutory voting is a voting procedure in which each shareholder is entitled to one vote per share, and votes must be divided evenly among the candidates being voted on.

83. C
The participant's retirement benefit in a defined contribution plan is based on the account balance. The account balance is affected by the investment performance. Pre-retirement inflation will likely affect salary levels and, therefore, affect the contribution amount. The participant's life expectancy does not directly affect the account balance in a defined contribution plan.

84. C
A closed-end mutual fund has a fixed number of shares that, after original issue, trade on the secondary market. The price an investor pays when buying shares of a closed-end mutual fund is based on supply and demand.

85. C
The times interest earned ratio is the measure of a company's ability to pay its debt obligations.

86. A
The date of declaration is the date that the board of directors approves and decides that a dividend will be paid.

87. C
The date of record is the date that it is determined who owns stock in the company and is entitled to receive a dividend.

88. B
The ex-dividend date is the date that the market price of the stock adjusts for the dividend.

89. D
A straddle is an option strategy that involves an investor holding a position in both a call and put for the same underlying security, with the same strike price and expiration date.

90. A
As a result of the SEC adopting an amendment to the Settlement Cycle Rule under the Securities Exchange Act of 1934, the standard settlement cycle was shortened from 3 business days after the trade (T+3) to 2 business days after the trade (T+2).

91. D
A federal gift tax return must be filed if a gift of a future interest is made, if spouses elect to split gifts, or if the gifts from a donor to any single donee for a calendar year exceed the amount of the gift tax annual exclusion.

92. C
SEC-registered investment advisers must deliver Form ADV Part 2A (brochure) and Part 2 (brochure supplement) to each client or prospective client.

93. D
The profitability ratios are the operating profit margin, net profit margin, return on assets, and return on equity.

94. B
Corporate investors in preferred stock can generally deduct 70% of the dividends they receive.

95. A
Deflation occurs when the supply of goods and services exceeds their demand.

96. C
The formula to calculate an investment's public offering price is: POP = NAV + Sales charge

97. C
A REMIC (real estate mortgage investment conduit) is a self-liquidating investment in real estate mortgages and mortgage-backed securities.

98. D
TRACE (Trade Reporting Compliance Engine) is the FINRA-developed vehicle that facilitates the mandatory reporting of over-the-counter secondary market transactions in eligible fixed income securities. All broker-dealers who are FINRA member firms have an obligation to report transactions in corporate bonds to TRACE under an SEC-approved set of rules.

99. B
GNP (gross national product) is the market value of all the goods and services produced in one year by labor and property supplied by the citizens of a country, wherever they are located.

100. C
According to Regulation D, firms may sell private placements to 35 non-accredited investors in a 12-month period.

101. D
The permitted distribution options from a qualified retirement plan are lump sum distribution, direct trustee-to-trustee transfer, payment in the form of an annuity or other periodic payment option, and rollover of funds from one qualified retirement plan to another.

102. B
A call is an option to buy a specified number of shares of stock during a specified period at a specified price. A buyer of a call option expects the price of the underlying stock to rise.

103. C
The underlying assumptions of the capital asset pricing model (CAPM) are that all investors have the same one-period time horizon, all investors have the same expectations about the risk-return relationship of assets, and there are no transaction costs, taxes, or inflation. The risk-free rate of return may be greater than zero.

104. B
According to FINRA's eligibility requirements, statutory disqualification will result for certain misdemeanors and all felony criminal convictions for a period of 10 years from the date of conviction.

105. C
A registration statement is a set of documents, including a prospectus, which a company must file with the SEC pursuant to the Securities Act of 1933 before it proceeds with a public offering.

106. B
Prospect theory suggests that investors typically fear losses more than they value gains. As a result, investors will often choose the smaller of two potential gains if it avoids a highly probable loss.

107. B
If interest rates decline following a bond issue, a sinking-fund provision will allow an issuing company to reduce the interest rate risk of its bonds as it replaces a portion of the existing debt with lower yielding bonds.

108. D
The yellow sheets are a daily publication of the National Quotation Bureau that details the bid and asked prices of corporate bonds traded in the over-the-counter market.

109. B
The efficient market hypothesis suggests that investors are unable to outperform the stock market on a consistent basis, the stock market's efficiency in valuing securities is rapid and accurate, and any excess returns are temporary and will regress to the mean. According to the efficient market hypothesis, daily fluctuations in stock prices are a result of a random walk pattern.

110. C
Book value = Total assets – Total liabilities
Book value = $3,250,000 – $2,980,000 = $270,000

111. B
A pooled income fund is generally created by a public charity, such as a private or public higher education institution or a not-for-profit hospital. In a pooled income fund, the donor's gifted property is commingled with property transferred by other donors, and additional contributions of property are permitted. A pooled income fund cannot invest in tax-exempt securities.

112. D
The goals of the Federal Reserve are to achieve full employment, minimize systematic risk, and stabilize prices.

113. C
A regressive tax is imposed in such a manner that the tax rate decreases as the amount subject to taxation increases.

114. D
The MSRB (Municipal Securities Rulemaking Board) has the mission of protecting investors, municipal entities, and the public interest by promoting a fair and efficient municipal market, regulating firms that engage in municipal securities and advisory activities, and promoting market transparency.

115. A
A large interest rate change has the most significant effect on a low coupon bond.

116. D
The assets ranked from most liquid to least liquid are Treasury bills, investment-grade corporate bonds, real estate, and the limited partnership.

117. A
ERISA requires retirement plan sponsors to disclose full and accurate information about qualified retirement plan activity to all participants.

118. B
Treasury STRIPS are always issued at a discount to par, like zero-coupon bonds.

119. B
Periodic interest payment = ($1,000 × 0.045) ÷ 2 = $22.50

120. B
In addition to the federal securities laws, each state has its own set of securities laws, commonly referred to as blue sky laws, which are designed to protect investors against fraudulent sales practices and activities.

121. A
With TIPS (treasury inflation-protected securities), investors are paid either the adjusted principal amount at maturity, or the original principal amount, whichever is greater. TIPS pay interest every six months, and their interest payments increase with inflation and decrease with deflation. They have maturities of 5, 10, or 30 years.

122. B
An FAC (face-amount certificate) is a contract between an investor and an issuer in which the issuer guarantees payment of a stated sum to the investor at some set date in the future. In return for this future payment, the investor agrees to pay the issuer a set amount of money either as a lump sum or in periodic installments.

123. B
Conduit theory states that an investment company that passes all capital gains, interest, and dividends through to its shareholders shouldn't be taxed at the corporate level.

124. C
A buy limit order is an order to purchase a security at or below a specified price.

125. B
Advertisements by an RIA include any notice, circular, or letter addressed to more than one person. It includes social media communications, such as Twitter feeds and online blogs. Advertisements are not permitted to use the initials "RIA" or "IAR."

126. D
The FDIC maintains stability and public confidence in the nation's financial system by insuring deposits, managing receiverships, and examining and supervising financial institutions for safety, soundness, and consumer protection. ERISA, not the FDIC, sets minimum standards for voluntarily established pension and health plans.

127. D
The Dodd-Frank Wall Street Reform and Consumer Protection Act of 2010 was intended to reshape the U.S. regulatory system in a number of areas including consumer protection, trading restrictions, credit ratings, regulation of financial products, corporate governance and disclosure, and transparency.

128. A
The smaller a bond's coupon, the greater its relative price fluctuation. The smaller a bond's coupon, the lower its reinvestment risk.

129. A
AMBAC (American Municipal Bond Assurance Corporation) insures the interest and principal payments for municipal bonds and other public finance debt obligations.

130. A
The annuity settlement options are cash, single life, life with period certain, joint-and-survivor, and installment refund.

PRACTICE EXAM 2

QUESTIONS

1. Congress has provided which of the following entities with the power to supervise self-regulatory organizations (SROs) as a matter of public interest?

   A. FINRA
   B. MSRB
   C. NASD
   D. SEC

2. In a short call, the maximum gain is _____ and the maximum loss is _____.

   A. unlimited, the premium paid
   B. the premium paid, unlimited
   C. unlimited, unlimited
   D. limited, limited

3. All but which of the following are correct regarding the Federal Open Market Committee (FOMC)?

   A. It consists of 12 members.
   B. It holds 8 regularly scheduled meetings per year.
   C. It reviews economic and financial conditions and determines the appropriate stance of monetary policy.
   D. All of the above are correct.

4. Which of the following acts is designed to promote the informed use of consumer credit by requiring disclosures about its terms and cost to standardize the manner in which costs associated with borrowing are calculated and disclosed?

   A. Uniform Securities Act of 1956
   B. Truth in Lending Act of 1968
   C. Securities Act Amendments of 1975
   D. Fair and Accurate Credit Transactions Act of 2003

5. Which of the following is/are correct regarding generation skipping transfers?

   (1) A taxable distribution occurs when a distribution is made to a skip person from a trust when a non-skip person still has an interest in the trust.
   (2) A skip person is a related individual one or more generations younger than the transferor.

   A. (1) only
   B. (2) only
   C. Both (1) and (2) are correct.
   D. Neither (1) or (2) are correct.

6. Regarding the money supply, which of the following is the formula for M3?

   A. M3 = M2 + Coins and currency in circulation + Money held in checking accounts
   B. M3 = M2 + Long-term time deposits
   C. M3 = M2 + Savings accounts + Short-term time deposits
   D. M3 = M2 – M1

7. Delta Corporation has retained earnings of $100,000, and they plan to use the funds to either invest in common stock or hire two new employees. Assuming these are mutually exclusive events, which of the following refers to the potential benefit that is lost by choosing one of these options over the other?

   A. Budget constraint
   B. Opportunity cost
   C. Production-possibility frontier
   D. Prospect theory

8. A special catch-up provision is permitted in 403(b) plans for employees with at least _____ of service who have not made contributions and are employed by universities.

   A. 5 years
   B. 10 years
   C. 15 years
   D. 20 years

9. Which of the following describes the maturities of Treasury bills, Treasury notes, and Treasury bonds?

   A. Treasury notes have maturities of 10 years or more.
   B. Treasury bills have maturities of 1 year or more.
   C. Treasury bonds have maturities greater than 10 years.
   D. All of the above are correct.

10. Jim, Mike, and Paul would each like to contribute money to their nephew's Coverdell Education Savings Account (ESA). Which of the following is correct regarding the maximum contribution that can be made on behalf of their nephew?

    A. Jim, Mike, and Paul are permitted to contribute a combined amount not to exceed $2,000 into their nephew's ESA in the current year.
    B. Jim, Mike, and Paul are permitted to each contribute $2,000 into their nephew's ESA in the current year, for a total annual contribution of $6,000.
    C. Jim, Mike, and Paul may each contribute up to the annual gift tax exclusion amount into their nephew's ESA in the current year.
    D. Jim, Mike, and Paul may "front-load" contributions into their nephew's ESA, so each may contribute up to five times the annual gift tax exclusion amount in the current year.

For questions 11 – 15, match the investment with the description that follows. Use only one answer per blank. Each answer may be used only once.

    A. Money market fund
    B. Corporate bond
    C. Common stock
    D. Mutual fund
    E. Real estate

11. ___ Diversification smooths price volatility, historical above-inflation return, can preserve purchasing power in a portfolio.

12. ___ Liquid, easily converted to cash, low default risk, low real return.

13. ___ Fixed return, may lose value if not held until maturity, fixed interest payments.

14. ___ Not liquid, generally adequate inflation hedge.

15. ___ Used to generate income and growth, marketable, historical above-inflation return, can preserve purchasing power in a portfolio.

16. Which of the following regulations governs private placement exemptions?

    A. Regulation A
    B. Regulation D
    C. Regulation T
    D. Regulation U

17. If an RIA has more than _____ of assets under management, the RIA must register with the SEC.

    A. $90 million
    B. $100 million
    C. $110 million
    D. $120 million

18. An investor sold short 25 shares of Omikron stock at a price of $98.50 per share. She also simultaneously placed a "good-till-cancelled, stop 102, limit 107 buy" order. Excluding transaction costs, what is the investor's maximum potential loss?

    A. $208.50
    B. $210.50
    C. $212.50
    D. $214.25

19. All but which of the following is another name for a balance sheet?

    A. Net worth statement
    B. Statement of assets and liabilities
    C. Statement of cash flows
    D. Statement of financial position

20. Christine purchased 100 shares of Alpha stock for $50 per share. At the end of two years, she sold the shares for $70 per share. In the first year, the stock did not pay a dividend. In the second year, the stock paid a $3 dividend. What was the holding period return of Christine's investment?

    A. 23%
    B. 26%
    C. 32%
    D. 46%

21. Which of the following acts was created in 2003 to prevent and mitigate identity theft, and includes a section that enables consumers to place fraud alerts in their credit files?

    A. FACT Act
    B. FAIR Act
    C. FICA Act
    D. FRAUD Act

22. Which of the following is correct regarding Keynesian economics?

    A. It is considered a "demand-side" theory that focuses on changes in the economy over the long run.
    B. It is considered a "demand-side" theory that focuses on changes in the economy over the short run.
    C. It is considered a "supply-side" theory that focuses on changes in the economy over the long run.
    D. It is considered a "supply-side" theory that focuses on changes in the economy over the short run.

23. Which of the following is the maximum civil penalty that can be imposed upon an individual who commits an insider trading violation?

    A. The civil penalty may be an amount up to two times the profit gained or the loss avoided as a result of the insider trading violation.
    B. The civil penalty may be an amount up to three times the profit gained or the loss avoided as a result of the insider trading violation.
    C. The civil penalty may be an amount up to $50,000.
    D. The civil penalty may be an amount up to $100,000.

24. Buying a _____ and selling a _____ are both bearish strategies.

    A. put, call
    B. put, put
    C. call, call
    D. call, put

For questions 25 – 28, match the stage of the business cycle with the description that follows. Use only one answer per blank. Answers may be used more than once or not at all.

    A. Trough
    B. Expansion
    C. Contraction
    D. Peak

25. ___ Recession

26. ___ Utilization at its lowest level

27. ___ Recovery

28. ___ GDP at its highest point

29. TIPS are indexed to the rate of inflation as measured by which of the following?

    A. Producer Price Index
    B. Personal Consumption Expenditures Price Index
    C. Implicit Price Deflator
    D. Consumer Price Index

30. Which of the following are correct regarding a bond's yield to maturity (YTM)?

    (1) The YTM assumes that coupon payments are reinvested at the YTM rate of return for the life of the bond.
    (2) When the market rate of interest for the same term and risk is higher than the coupon rate, a discount will be priced into the bond.
    (3) Bonds that are riskier will have lower yields to maturity.
    (4) The YTM is the internal rate of return for cash flow associated with a bond, including the purchase price, coupon payments, and maturity value.

    A. (1) and (2) only
    B. (3) and (4) only
    C. (1), (2), and (4) only
    D. (1), (3), and (4) only

31. According to the Uniform Securities Act, all but which of the following are methods of registering securities offerings in a state?

A. Registration by coordination
B. Registration by notification
C. Registration by origination
D. Registration by qualification

32. A mutual fund that invests in securities both inside and outside the U.S. is known as which of the following?

A. Arbitrage fund
B. Global fund
C. International fund
D. Long-short fund

33. In order to withdraw registration as an investment adviser, an individual must file which of the following?

A. Form ADV-BR
B. Form ADV-E
C. Form ADV-H
D. Form ADV-W

34. Which of the following is the prohibited practice of entering into an equity trade to capitalize on advance, nonpublic knowledge of a large pending transaction that will influence the price of the underlying security?

A. Capping
B. Front running
C. Painting the tape
D. Pegging

35. According to the Telephone Consumer Protection Act, companies must maintain do-not-call lists reflecting the names of customers who have requested to be excluded from telemarketing, and those requests must be honored for how many years?

A. 1 year
B. 2 years
C. 5 years
D. 7 years

36. The duration of a coupon bond is always _____ its term to maturity. A zero-coupon bond's duration is always _____ its term to maturity.

A. equal to, less than
B. greater than, less than
C. less than, greater than
D. less than, equal to

37. Which of the following acts mandated a number of reforms to enhance corporate responsibility, enhance financial disclosures, and combat corporate and accounting fraud? It also created the "Public Company Accounting Oversight Board," to oversee the activities of the auditing profession.

    A. National Securities Market Improvement Act of 1996
    B. Patriot Act of 2001
    C. Sarbanes-Oxley Act of 2002
    D. Dodd-Frank Wall Street Reform and Consumer Protection Act of 2010

38. Which of the following provides the decedent/grantor's estate with the unlimited marital deduction while, at the same time, ensuring that the decedent retains control over the ultimate disposition of his or her property?

    A. Marital trust
    B. Credit shelter trust
    C. QTIP trust
    D. Revocable trust

39. How frequently will a mutual fund with a turnover ratio of 20% replace its total holdings?

    A. Every year
    B. Every 2 years
    C. Every 4 years
    D. Every 5 years

40. Which of the following refers to using property to secure payment of a loan, which includes mortgages, pledges, and putting up collateral, but the borrower retains possession?

    A. Hypothecate
    B. Pledge
    C. Remunerate
    D. None of the above are correct.

41. All but which of the following are correct regarding FINRA's emergency preparedness rule?

    A. A firm must disclose to its customers how its business continuity plan addresses the possibility of a significant business disruption and how the firm plans to respond to events of varying scope.
    B. A firm's business continuity plan must be made available promptly to FINRA staff if requested.
    C. A firm's business continuity plan must be reasonably designed so the firm can meet its existing obligations to customers.
    D. A firm's business continuity plan may be kept confidential from clients.

42. Which of the following is the central banking system of the United States?

   A. Federal Reserve
   B. FOMC
   C. U.S. Mint
   D. U.S. Treasury

43. Which of the following acts requires trustees to follow the modern portfolio theory of investing?

   A. Uniform Securities Act of 1956
   B. Securities Investor Protection Act of 1970
   C. Uniform Prudent Investor Act of 1994
   D. National Securities Market Improvement Act of 1996

44. William, age 56, recently retired from Epsilon Inc., and would like to take a distribution from a retirement plan to pay for medical expenses. Which of the following plans would allow William to take a penalty free withdrawal?

   A. Single premium deferred annuity
   B. Traditional IRA
   C. Money purchase plan from his employer before Epsilon Inc.
   D. 401(k) from Epsilon Inc.

45. Which of the following is a type of bond offered as a tranche class of some CMOs, according to a sinking-fund schedule?

   A. General obligation bond
   B. Planned amortization class (PAC) bond
   C. Targeted amortization class (TAC) bond
   D. Zero-coupon bond

46. Which of the following is an unconditional contract between a bond issuer and a bondholder that specifies the terms of the bond?

   A. Debenture
   B. Indenture
   C. Prospectus
   D. Tombstone ad

47. Futures trading is regulated by which of the following?

   A. AMBAC
   B. CFTC
   C. NASAA
   D. OCC

48. Alpha Corporation reports the following information for the fiscal year (in millions):

Revenue	$6,115
Expenses	$3,770
Beginning retained earnings	$510
Liabilities at year-end	$985
Contributed capital at year-end	$440
Dividends	$0
Effective tax rate	35%

What is the value of Alpha Corporation's total assets at year-end?

A. $1,935 million
B. $3,260 million
C. $4,280 million
D. $8,050 million

49. Which of the following represents the maximum amount of capital loss that an individual taxpayer can deduct in a single year?

A. Up to the amount of capital gain.
B. Up to the amount of capital gain plus $3,000.
C. Up to the amount of capital gain plus $6,000.
D. Only $3,000.

50. Which of the following is referred to as the "know your customer" rule, which states that a customer's situation must be suitable for any investment being made?

A. Securities Act Rule 144
B. Securities Act Rule 405
C. Securities Act Rule 433
D. Securities Act Rule 506

51. All but which of the following are charting techniques used by technical analysts?

A. CAPM
B. Moving average
C. Support and resistance levels
D. Trendline

52. The Dow Jones Utility Average is an index comprised of _____ utility stocks.

A. 15
B. 30
C. 50
D. 100

53. All but which of the following are characteristics of tangible assets, such as collectibles?

    A. They do not have a strong secondary market.
    B. They are not subject to significant government regulation.
    C. They are marketable.
    D. They lack liquidity.

54. Which of the following forms must broker-dealers, investment advisers, or issuers of securities fill out in order to terminate the registration of an individual in the appropriate jurisdiction? It is also known as the Uniform Termination Notice for Securities Industry Registration.

    A. Form U4
    B. Form U5
    C. Form U6
    D. Form U7

55. Earnings after taxes ÷ Annual sales = _____

    A. Average collection period
    B. Net profit margin
    C. Operating profit margin
    D. Quick ratio

For questions 56 – 59, match the charitable trust with the description that follows. Use only one answer per blank. Answers may be used more than once or not at all.

    A. Charitable remainder annuity trust (CRAT)
    B. Charitable remainder unitrust (CRUT)
    C. Neither A or B
    D. Both A and B

56. ___ Income tax savings, income is a sum certain

57. ___ Income tax savings, income can be provided for life

58. ___ Income tax savings, immediate income to charity

59. ___ Estate tax savings, income is variable

60. An investment-grade bond is one that is rated _____ or higher by Moody's. A high-yield bond is rated _____ or lower by Moody's.

    A. Ba, Baa
    B. Baa, Ba
    C. Baa3, Ba1
    D. Baa+, Ba-

61. Which of the following forms must companies file with the SEC to announce certain material events or corporate changes that shareholders should be made aware of?

    A. Form 8-K
    B. Form 10-K
    C. Form 10-Q
    D. Form I-9

62. The S&P index has _____ risk.

    A. non-systematic
    B. non-diversifiable
    C. diversifiable
    D. unsystematic

63. Which of the following is the system for reporting and clearing trades in the over-the-counter (OTC) and NASDAQ securities markets?

    A. Automated Confirmation Transaction Service
    B. Automated Quotation Service
    C. Automated National Transaction Service
    D. Automated OTC Clearing Service

64. Beta Corporation reports the following information for the fiscal year:

Revenue	$2,875,000
Cost of goods sold	$1,950,000
Return of goods sold	$160,000
Cash collected	$1,425,000
Effective tax rate	30%

    According to the accrual basis of accounting, what is Beta Corporation's reported net revenue?

    A. $925,000
    B. $1,085,000
    C. $1,585,000
    D. $2,715,000

65. Which of the following is correct regarding IRA contributions?

    A. IRA contributions made above the maximum annual limit are subject to a 10% nondeductible excise tax.
    B. A nonworking divorced person, age 40, who receives alimony may contribute to an IRA the lesser of the maximum contribution limit or 100% of the alimony received.
    C. An employee who makes voluntary contributions to a 401(k) plan is not considered an active participant for the purpose of making IRA contributions.
    D. An employee participating in a 457 plan is considered an active participant for the purpose of making IRA contributions.

66. Which of the following help to facilitate block trading and are known for their lack of transparency?

A. Blind trusts
B. Dark pools
C. Pooled income funds
D. Private placements

67. Which of the following is the governing body of FINRA, which oversees the administration of its affairs and the promotion of its welfare, objectives, and purposes?

A. Board of Governors
B. Board of Trustees
C. Congress
D. FINRA Chairman

68. Which of the following are correct regarding exchange-traded funds (ETFs)?

(1) Unlike mutual funds, investors can buy and sell ETFs throughout the trading day.
(2) ETFs can be bought on margin or sold short.
(3) There is never a transaction fee to buy or sell an ETF.
(4) ETFs have low management fees compared to mutual funds.

A. (3) only
B. (4) only
C. (1), (2), and (3) only
D. (1), (2), and (4) only

69. All but which of the following are correct regarding the stock market trading pattern known as "sector rotation"?

A. It involves shifting investments from one sector of the economy to another.
B. It is a passive investment strategy, similar to indexing.
C. It assumes that sector performance is correlated to the business cycle.
D. It can be expensive to implement because of the potential costs associated with extensive trading activity.

70. All but which of the following statements are correct regarding bonds and preferred stock?

A. If a company declares bankruptcy, bondholders are repaid before preferred stock shareholders.
B. Preferred stocks pay dividends; bonds pay interest.
C. Bonds are subject to greater interest rate risk than preferred stock.
D. Neither bond interest nor preferred stock dividends qualify for capital gains treatment.

71. A share of Omega preferred stock has a par value of $100 and a preferred dividend rate of 6.25%. If the required return is 11.5%, what is the price per share?

A. $54.35
B. $98.50
C. $184.00
D. $196.00

72. All but which of the following are types of municipal bonds?

A. General obligation bond
B. Preferred bond
C. Private activity bond
D. Revenue bond

For questions 73 – 76, determine if the exchange described qualifies as a 1035 exchange. Use only one answer per blank. Answers may be used more than once or not at all.

A. 1035 exchange
B. Not a 1035 exchange

73. ___ A life insurance policy exchanged for a life insurance policy.

74. ___ An annuity exchanged for an annuity.

75. ___ An annuity exchanged for a life insurance policy.

76. ___ A life insurance policy exchanged for an annuity.

77. All but which of the following are correct regarding an "unqualified opinion"?

A. It is an independent auditor's judgment that a company's financial reports are fairly and appropriately presented.
B. It is considered to be a "clean" auditor's report.
C. It is also known as a "disclaimer of opinion."
D. It indicates that the financial reports conform to GAAP.

78. Which of the following is/are correct regarding the early withdrawal penalty from a SIMPLE IRA?

(1) Early withdrawals are subject to a 20% penalty if the withdrawals are made during the first two years of plan participation.
(2) After the initial two-year period, early withdrawals from a SIMPLE IRA are subject to a 10% penalty.

A. (1) only
B. (2) only
C. Both (1) and (2) are correct.
D. Neither (1) or (2) are correct.

79. Which of the following yield curves results from short-term debt instruments having a lower yield than long-term debt instruments of the same credit quality?

    A. Flat yield curve
    B. Inverted yield curve
    C. Normal yield curve
    D. Steep yield curve

80. Which of the following is a manipulative trading activity that is designed to prevent the price of a security from falling?

    A. Capping
    B. Front running
    C. Painting the tape
    D. Pegging

81. The Securities Acts Amendments of 1975 did which of the following?

    A. It gave authority to the Municipal Securities Rulemaking Board (MSRB).
    B. It required financial institutions to assist U.S. government agencies to detect and prevent money laundering.
    C. It provided fiduciary responsibilities for those who manage and control plan assets and gave participants the right to sue for benefits and breaches of fiduciary duty.
    D. It created the Public Company Accounting Oversight Board to oversee the activities of the auditing profession.

82. A security has an expected annual return of 9.5% and an expected standard deviation of 14.4%. The market has an expected annual return of 7.8% and an expected standard deviation of 12.2. If the correlation between the security and the market is 0.75, what is the security's beta?

    A. 0.64
    B. 0.89
    C. 1.02
    D. 1.09

83. Which of the following anomalies support the efficient market hypothesis?

    (1) The January Effect
    (2) The Neglected Firm Effect
    (3) The Turn-of-the-Month Effect
    (4) The Value Line Anomaly

    A. (1) and (3) only
    B. (2) and (3) only
    C. All of the above support the efficient market hypothesis.
    D. None of the above support the efficient market hypothesis.

84. Which of the following is correct regarding the taxation of qualified dividends?

    A. They are taxed as ordinary income.
    B. They are exempt from taxation.
    C. They are taxed at the long-term capital gains tax rate.
    D. They are taxed at the short-term capital gains tax rate.

85. A nonexempt unregistered security may be sold through with of the following?

    A. Common stock
    B. IPO
    C. Mutual fund
    D. Private placement

86. Which of the following is a characteristic of American Depository Receipts (ADRs)?

    A. ADRs trade once per day like mutual funds.
    B. ADR holders receive foreign tax credits for income tax paid to a foreign country.
    C. ADR dividends are declared in U.S. dollars.
    D. ADRs allow domestic securities to be traded in foreign countries.

87. All but which of the following information is commonly found in a mutual fund prospectus?

    A. Fees and expenses
    B. Investment objectives
    C. Principal risks of investing in the fund
    D. All of the above are correct.

88. Which of the following is the formula to calculate gross national product (GNP)?

    A. GDP + Net income inflow from abroad − Net income outflow to foreign countries
    B. GDP + Net income inflow from abroad + Net income outflow to foreign countries
    C. GDP − Net income inflow from abroad − Net income outflow to foreign countries
    D. GDP − Net income inflow from abroad + Net income outflow to foreign countries

89. Which of the following are dollar-denominated bonds issued by emerging markets (typically Latin American countries) and collateralized by U.S. Treasuries?

    A. Brady bonds
    B. Eurobonds
    C. Fidelity bonds
    D. Surety bonds

90. According to the "brochure rule," investment advisers must deliver the brochure to clients not less than _____ prior to entering into any written or oral investment advisory contract, or no later than the time of entering into such contract if the client has the right to terminate the contract without penalty within _____ after entering into the contract.

    A. 24 hours, 2 business days
    B. 24 hours, 5 business days
    C. 48 hours, 2 business days
    D. 48 hours, 5 business days

91. Which of the following entities is subject to double taxation?

    A. C Corp
    B. S Corp
    C. LLC
    D. Partnership

92. Under the provisions of ERISA, a fiduciary is an individual who meets which of the following criteria?

    (1) Exercises discretionary authority over retirement plan management.
    (2) Has discretionary authority or responsibility over plan administration.
    (3) Renders investment advice for a fee or other compensation.
    (4) Exercises authority or control over the disposition of retirement plan assets.

    A. (1) and (3) only
    B. (2) and (4) only
    C. (1), (2), and (4) only
    D. All of the above are correct.

93. All but which of the following are correct regarding stock market benchmarks and indexes?

    A. The NASDAQ Composite is a value-weighted index.
    B. The Russell 2000 is a value-weighted index.
    C. The S&P 500 is a price-weighted index.
    D. The Wilshire 5000 is a value-weighted index.

94. The standard expiration period for a put or call option is _____. Long-term equity anticipation securities (LEAPS) have an expiration period _____.

    A. 6 months, longer than 1 year
    B. 6 months, between 6 months and 1 year
    C. 9 months, between 9 months and 1 year
    D. 9 months, longer than 1 year

95. Incentive stock options (ISOs) may be granted to which of the following?

    A. Employees
    B. Independent contractors
    C. Non-employee directors
    D. All of the above are correct.

96. Which of the following is a type of exchange rate system in which a country ties its currency to a basket of other currencies or to another measure of value, such as gold?

    A. Adjustable exchange rate system
    B. Commodity exchange rate system
    C. Fixed exchange rate system
    D. Variable exchange rate system

97. Monetary policy is carried out through all but which of the following methods?

    A. Open market operations
    B. Changing the discount rate
    C. Changing the reserve requirements
    D. Taxation

98. Beta Corporation provides the following information in its annual shareholder report:

Net income	$660,000
Depreciation	$35,000
Increase in accounts receivable	$110,000
Increase in accounts payable	$120,000

    What is Beta Corporation's cash flow from operations?

    A. $685,000
    B. $705,000
    C. $890,000
    D. $925,000

99. Which of the following U.S. Supreme Court cases defined an investment contract as "a contract, transaction, or scheme whereby a person invests his money in a common enterprise and is led to expect profits solely from the efforts of the promoter or a third party"?

    A. Securities and Exchange Commission v. Edwards
    B. Securities and Exchange Commission v. Ralston Purina Co.
    C. Securities and Exchange Commission v. Plexcorps
    D. Securities and Exchange Commission v. W. J. Howey Co.

100. An investor sells a naked call on Omikron for a $250 premium. Which of the following is true regarding the investor's position?

    A. The investor is expecting Omikron stock to increase in value.
    B. The investor's potential loss is unlimited.
    C. The investor's potential loss is limited to $250.
    D. The investor's outlook for Omikron stock is bullish.

101. If Zeta Fund's Sharpe ratio is 0.76, its standard deviation is 9%, and the risk free-rate is 3.5%, what is the fund's return?

    A. 9.92%
    B. 10.34%
    C. 10.56%
    D. 10.72%

102. Which of the following passes capital gains, dividends, and interest earned on fund investments directly to shareholders so that it is taxed only at the personal level, and double taxation is avoided?

    A. Private placement
    B. Regulated investment company
    C. Unregulated investment company
    D. Wholly owned subsidiary

103. Which of the following is a form of insurance protection that covers public consumers for losses that they incur as a result of fraudulent acts by specified individuals, such as employees of a broker-dealer?

    A. Brady bond
    B. Debenture bond
    C. Fidelity bond
    D. Surety bond

104. On September 12th of last year, Joel bought 100 shares of Sigma stock for $20 per share. On December 18th of last year, he sold all of his shares for $1,600. On January 3rd of this year, Joel bought back 100 shares of Sigma stock for $20 per share. Which of the following is true regarding Joel's transaction?

    A. Joel can realize the $400 loss.
    B. If Joel waited a few more days to buy back the stock, he could have realized the gain.
    C. The wash sale rule doesn't apply to Joel because the transactions occurred in two separate years.
    D. No loss deduction is allowed; the amount of the disallowed loss will be added to the cost basis of the shares that Joel purchased on January 3rd.

105. Which of the following is required by the IRS if a taxpayer uses the substantially equal periodic payment (SEPP) exception to the premature distribution penalty?

   A. The taxpayer must show proof of economic hardship.
   B. The taxpayer must show proof that payments will be used to pay for qualified medical or education expenses.
   C. The taxpayer must show proof that appropriate taxes will be withheld.
   D. None of the above are correct.

106. Kate owns an investment yielding an 18% pre-tax return. If she is in the 28% tax bracket, what is the equivalent after-tax return?

   A. 5.04%
   B. 12.96%
   C. 14.28%
   D. 23.04%

107. Based on the Markowitz efficient frontier model, which of the following securities would a rational investor select?

   A. Security A has a 5% rate of return and a beta of 0.8.
   B. Security B has a 6% rate of return and a beta of 0.8.
   C. Security C has a 3% rate of return and a beta of 0.7.
   D. Security D has a 6% rate of return and a beta of 0.6.

108. Which of the following is the result of persistent high inflation combined with high unemployment and a slowing demand for goods and services?

   A. Deflation
   B. Inflation
   C. Reflation
   D. Stagflation

109. Which of the following is/are correct regarding profit sharing plans?

   (1) Contributions to a profit sharing plan may not be skewed to favor older employees.
   (2) The allocation formula may discriminate in favor of highly compensated employees.

   A. (1) only
   B. (2) only
   C. Both (1) and (2) are correct.
   D. Neither (1) or (2) are correct.

110. **The Alpha and Treynor ratios assume a _____ portfolio. The Sharpe ratio assumes a _____ portfolio.**

    A. diversified, non-diversified
    B. non-diversified, diversified
    C. non-diversified, riskless
    D. riskless, diversified

111. **The two broad categories of defined contribution plans are:**

    A. defined benefit plans and pension plans.
    B. personal plans and employer plans.
    C. profit sharing plans and pension plans.
    D. qualified plans and profit sharing plans.

112. **All but which of the following are correct regarding a UGMA/UTMA account?**

    A. Unlike a 529 plan, funds do not need to be used to pay for education expenses.
    B. The custodian, typically the minor's parent, does not own the assets in the account.
    C. Similar to a 529 plan, funds in the account grow tax-deferred.
    D. Once the account is set up, it's considered to be an irrevocable gift.

113. **According to SEC Rule 506(b), private placements may be sold to how many accredited and non-accredited investors?**

    A. An unlimited number of accredited investors and up to 35 non-accredited investors.
    B. An unlimited number of accredited investors and up to 100 non-accredited investors.
    C. A total of 35 accredited and non-accredited investors.
    D. A total of 100 investors, of which 35 can be non-accredited.

114. **Which of the following is the penalty for a premature distribution from a qualified plan, 403(b) plan, IRA, or SEP?**

    A. 5%
    B. 10%
    C. 15%
    D. Ordinary income tax rates

115. **As bond interest rates _____, bond duration _____.**

    A. decrease, decreases
    B. decrease, increases
    C. increase, increases
    D. increase, is unchanged

116. If real GDP declined last quarter, how many more consecutive quarters of decline would be needed to be classified as an economic recession?

    A. 1 quarter
    B. 2 quarters
    C. 3 quarters
    D. 4 quarters

117. Which of the following describes bonds that have a legal claim to specific assets in the event of default, insolvency, or liquidation?

    A. Debenture bonds
    B. Indenture bonds
    C. Secured bonds
    D. Unsecured bonds

118. Which of the following goods decrease in demand as consumer income increases?

    A. Inferior good
    B. Normal good
    C. Superior good
    D. None of the above are correct.

119. Which of the following is correct regarding a pre-emptive right?

    A. It is also referred to as a "subscription right" or a "subscription privilege."
    B. It is an obligation for existing shareholders to purchase new shares of stock before they are offered to the public.
    C. Exercising a pre-emptive right can cause dilution.
    D. All of the above are correct.

120. Hybrid REITs combine features of which of the following?

    A. Equity REITs and commodity REITs
    B. Equity REITs and mortgage REITs
    C. Mortgage REITs and commodity REITs
    D. None of the above are correct.

121. Which of the following refers to the high-speed electronic system that reports the latest price and volume data on sales of exchange-listed stocks?

    A. Consolidated tape
    B. Instinet
    C. EDGAR
    D. TRACE

The following information relates to questions 122 – 123.

Theta Inc. provides the following information on their year-end financial statement:

Cash and cash equivalents	$150,000
Short-term marketable securities	$90,000
Receivables	$195,000
Other non-financial assets	$65,000
Current liabilities	$200,000
Non-current liabilities	$40,000

122. **What is Theta Inc.'s quick ratio?**

    A. 2.08
    B. 2.18
    C. 2.50
    D. 2.72

123. **What is Theta Inc.'s cash ratio?**

    A. 0.63
    B. 1.00
    C. 1.20
    D. 1.30

124. **All but which of the following are correct regarding solicitors?**

    A. Being a "solicitor" typically involves soliciting, referring, offering, or negotiating the sale of investment advisory services on behalf of a third party financial adviser for monetary compensation.
    B. According to SEC Rule 206(4)-3, the terms of the fee to be paid and solicitor activity being conducted must be documented by a written agreement.
    C. Both individuals and entities can be considered solicitors.
    D. Individuals that merely solicit on behalf of an RIA firm are never required to qualify as an individual IAR or establish his or her own investment advisory firm.

125. **Which of the following acts applies to debt securities, such as bonds, debentures, and notes that are offered for public sale? Even though such securities may be registered under the Securities Act, they may not be offered for sale to the public unless a formal agreement between the issuer of bonds and the bondholder conforms to the standards of this act.**

    A. Maloney Act of 1938
    B. Trust Indenture Act of 1939
    C. Investment Company Act of 1940
    D. Securities Investor Protection Act of 1970

126. Dennis, a Vice President at Gamma Corporation, earns $450,000 in 2018. If the company has installed a 15% money purchase plan, how much can the company contribute on his behalf?

   A. $18,500
   B. $41,250
   C. $55,000
   D. $67,500

127. Regarding municipal bonds, which of the following is the small amount of money, usually less than 5% of an issue, that underwriters give to the issuer in exchange for the right to place part of the issue?

   A. Credit deposit
   B. Down payment
   C. Escrow deposit
   D. Good faith deposit

128. A fixed income security is subject to which of the following risks?

   (1) Exchange rate risk
   (2) Purchasing power risk
   (3) Default risk
   (4) Liquidity risk
   (5) Reinvestment risk

   A. (1), (2), (3), and (4) only
   B. (1), (2), (4), and (5) only
   C. (2), (3), (4), and (5) only
   D. All of the above are correct.

129. Which of the following refers to direct institution-to-institution trading, usually done in blocks, without using the service of broker-dealers?

   A. First market
   B. Second market
   C. Third market
   D. Fourth market

130. Which of the following acts established the policies and procedures commonly referred to as a "Chinese wall"?

   A. Uniform Securities Act of 1956
   B. Bank Secrecy Act of 1970
   C. Insider Trading and Securities Fraud Enforcement Act of 1988
   D. Sarbanes-Oxley Act of 2002

ANSWER KEY

1. D
Congress has provided the SEC with the power to supervise self-regulatory organizations (SROs) as a matter of public interest.

2. B
In a short call, the maximum gain is the premium paid and the maximum loss is unlimited.

3. D
The Federal Open Market Committee (FOMC) consists of 12 members and holds 8 regularly scheduled meetings per year. It reviews economic and financial conditions and determines the appropriate stance of monetary policy.

4. B
The Truth in Lending Act of 1968 is designed to promote the informed use of consumer credit by requiring disclosures about its terms and cost to standardize the manner in which costs associated with borrowing are calculated and disclosed.

5. A
A taxable distribution occurs when a distribution is made to a skip person from a trust when a non-skip person still has an interest in the trust. A skip person is a related individual two or more generations younger than the transferor.

6. B
M3 = M2 + Long-term time deposits

7. B
The potential benefit that is lost by choosing one option over another is referred to as the opportunity cost.

8. C
A special catch-up provision is permitted in 403(b) plans for employees with at least 15 years of service who have not made contributions and are employed by universities.

9. C
Treasury bills have maturities of 1 year or less.
Treasury notes have maturities of 10 years or less.
Treasury bonds have maturities greater than 10 years.

10. A
Coverdell Education Savings Accounts (ESAs) have a maximum contribution limit of $2,000 per beneficiary per year.

11. D
Mutual fund: Diversification smooths price volatility, historical above-inflation return, can preserve purchasing power in a portfolio.

12. A
Money market fund: Liquid, easily converted to cash, low default risk, low real return.

13. B
Corporate bond: Fixed return, may lose value if not held until maturity, fixed interest payments.

14. E
Real estate: Not liquid, generally adequate inflation hedge.

15. C
Common stock: Used to generate income and growth, marketable, historical above-inflation return, can preserve purchasing power in a portfolio.

16. B
Regulation D governs private placement exemptions.

17. C
If an RIA has more than $110 million of assets under management, the RIA must register with the SEC.

18. C
($107 – $98.50) × 25 shares = $212.50

19. C
A balance sheet can also be referred to as a net worth statement, statement of assets and liabilities, and statement of financial position.

20. D
HPR = [($7,000 + $300) – $5,000] ÷ $5,000 = 0.46 = 46%

21. A
The FACT Act (Fair and Accurate Credit Transactions Act) was created in 2003 to prevent and mitigate identity theft and includes a section that enables consumers to place fraud alerts in their credit files.

22. B
Keynesian economics is considered a "demand-side" theory that focuses on changes in the economy over the short run.

23. B
The civil penalty may be an amount up to three times the profit gained or the loss avoided as a result of the insider trading violation.

24. A
Buying a put and selling a call are both bearish strategies.

25. C
The contraction stage of the business cycle is characterized by recession.

26. A
At the trough of the business cycle, utilization will be at its lowest level.

27. B
The expansion stage of the business cycle is characterized by recovery.

28. D
At the peak of the business cycle, GDP will be at its highest point.

29. D
TIPS (treasury inflation-protected securities) are indexed to the rate of inflation as measured by the Consumer Price Index (CPI).

30. C
The yield to maturity (YTM) is the internal rate of return for cash flow associated with a bond, including the purchase price, coupon payments, and maturity value. It assumes that coupon payments are reinvested at the YTM rate of return for the life of the bond. When the market rate of interest for the same term and risk is higher than the coupon rate, a discount will be priced into the bond. Bonds that are riskier will have higher yields to maturity.

31. C
According to the Uniform Securities Act, the methods of registering securities offerings in a state are registration by coordination, registration by notification, and registration by qualification.

32. B
A mutual fund that invests in securities both inside and outside the U.S. is known as a global fund.

33. D
In order to withdraw registration as an investment adviser, an individual must file Form ADV-W.

34. B
Front running is the prohibited practice of entering into an equity trade to capitalize on advance, nonpublic knowledge of a large pending transaction that will influence the price of the underlying security.

35. C
According to the Telephone Consumer Protection Act, companies must maintain do-not-call lists reflecting the names of customers who have requested to be excluded from tele-marketing. Such requests must be honored for 5 years.

36. D
The duration of a coupon bond is always less than its term to maturity. A zero-coupon bond's duration is always equal to its term to maturity.

37. C
The Sarbanes-Oxley Act of 2002 mandated a number of reforms to enhance corporate responsibility, enhance financial disclosures, and combat corporate and accounting fraud. It also created the "Public Company Accounting Oversight Board," to oversee the activities of the auditing profession.

38. C
A QTIP trust provides the decedent/grantor's estate with the unlimited marital deduction while, at the same time, ensuring that the decedent retains control over the ultimate disposition of his or her property.

39. D
$1 \div 0.20 = 5$
A mutual fund with a turnover ratio of 20% will replace its total holdings every 5 years.

40. A
Hypothecate refers to using property to secure payment of a loan, which includes mortgages, pledges, and putting up collateral, but the borrower retains possession.

41. D
According to FINRA's emergency preparedness rule, a firm must disclose to its customers how its business continuity plan addresses the possibility of a significant business disruption and how the firm plans to respond to events of varying scope. A firm's business continuity plan must be made available promptly to FINRA staff if requested, and it must be reasonably designed so the firm can meet its existing obligations to customers. The plan must be made in writing to customers when they open their account, posted on the firm's website if they maintain one, and mailed to customers upon request.

42. A
The Federal Reserve is the central banking system of the United States.

43. C
The Uniform Prudent Investor Act of 1994 requires trustees to follow the modern portfolio theory of investing.

44. D
Withdrawals from a 401(k) after separating from service are penalty free if the separation occurs at age 55 or older. The other options would result in an early withdrawal penalty.

45. C
A targeted amortization class (TAC) bond is a type of bond offered as a tranche class of some CMOs, according to a sinking-fund schedule.

46. B
An indenture is an unconditional contract between a bond issuer and a bondholder that specifies the terms of the bond.

47. B
Futures trading is regulated by the Commodity Futures Trading Commission (CFTC).

48. C

Assets = Liabilities at year-end + Contributed capital at year-end + Beginning retained earnings + Revenues – Expenses – Dividends

Assets = $985 + $440 + $510 + $6,115 – $3,770 = $4,280 million

49. B

The maximum amount of capital loss that an individual taxpayer can deduct in a single year is up to the amount of capital gain plus $3,000.

50. B

Securities Act Rule 405 is referred to as the "know your customer" rule, which states that a customer's situation must be suitable for any investment being made.

51. A

Technical analysts use charting techniques which include the moving average, support and resistance levels, and trendline.

52. A

The Dow Jones Utility Average is an index comprised of 15 utility stocks.

53. C

Collectibles lack marketability and liquidity. They do not have a strong secondary market and they're not subject to significant government regulation.

54. B

Broker-dealers, investment advisers, and issuers of securities must fill out form U5 in order to terminate the registration of an individual in the appropriate jurisdiction. It is also known as the Uniform Termination Notice for Securities Industry Registration.

55. B

Earnings after taxes ÷ Annual sales = Net profit margin

56. A

A charitable remainder annuity trust (CRAT) provides fixed income that is a sum certain.

57. D

Both a charitable remainder annuity trust (CRAT) and charitable remainder unitrust (CRUT) can provide income to the grantor for life, along with a deduction for the charitable contribution of the remainder interest.

58. C

Neither a charitable remainder annuity trust (CRAT) nor charitable remainder unitrust (CRUT) provides immediate income to charity. Instead, they provide an interest to charity after income has been paid to the grantor. A charitable lead trust provides immediate income to charity.

59. B

A charitable remainder unitrust (CRUT) provides variable income because the income is based on the value of the trust assets revalued annually.

60. C

An investment-grade bond is one that is rated Baa3 or higher by Moody's. A high-yield bond is rated Ba1 or lower by Moody's.

61. A

Companies must file Form 8-K with the SEC to announce certain material events or corporate changes that shareholders should be made aware of.

62. B

The S&P index has systematic risk only. Systematic risk is also referred to as non-diversifiable risk. The other answers (non-systematic risk, diversifiable risk, and unsystematic risk) all refer to the same type of risk.

63. A

The Automated Confirmation Transaction Service (ACT) is the system for reporting and clearing trades in the over-the-counter (OTC) and NASDAQ securities markets.

64. D

Net revenue = Revenue – Returns and adjustments
Net revenue = $2,875,000 – $160,000 = $2,715,000

65. B

The nondeductible excise tax for over-contributing to an IRA is 6%, not 10%. An employee who makes voluntary contributions to a 401(k) plan is considered an active participant. However, an employee participating in a 457 plan is not an active participant. A nonworking divorced person, age 40, who receives alimony may contribute to an IRA the lesser of the maximum contribution limit or 100% of the alimony received.

66. B

Dark pools help to facilitate block trading and are known for their lack of transparency.

67. A

The Board of Governors is the governing body of FINRA and oversees the administration of its affairs and the promotion of its welfare, objectives, and purposes.

68. D

Unlike mutual funds, investors can buy and sell exchange-traded funds (ETFs) throughout the trading day. ETFs can be bought on margin or sold short, and they carry low management fees because they require very little active management. There is typically a transaction fee any time an ETF is bought or sold.

69. B

Sector rotation involves shifting investments from one sector of the economy to another. It assumes that sector performance is correlated to the business cycle, and it can be expensive to implement because of the potential costs associated with extensive trading activity. It is an active investment strategy, not passive.

70. C
Preferred stock does not have a fixed maturity date. Therefore, it has unlimited interest rate risk. If a company declares bankruptcy, bondholders are repaid before preferred stock shareholders. Preferred stocks pay dividends; bonds pay interest. Neither bond interest nor preferred stock dividends qualify for capital gains treatment.

71. A
$P_p = D_p \div r_p$
$P_p = (0.0625 \times \$100) \div 0.115 = \$54.35$

72. B
Types of municipal bonds include general obligation bonds, private activity bonds, and revenue bonds.

73. A
A life insurance policy exchanged for a life insurance policy is a permitted 1035 exchange.

74. A
An annuity exchanged for an annuity is a permitted 1035 exchange.

75. B
An annuity exchanged for a life insurance policy is not a permitted 1035 exchange.

76. A
A life insurance policy exchanged for an annuity is a permitted 1035 exchange.

77. C
An unqualified opinion is an independent auditor's judgment that a company's financial reports are fairly and appropriately presented. It is considered to be a "clean" auditor's report, and it indicates that the financial reports conform to GAAP.

78. B
Early withdrawals from a SIMPLE IRA are subject to a 25% penalty if the withdrawals are made during the first two years of plan participation. After the initial two-year period, the early withdrawal penalty is reduced to 10%.

79. C
A normal yield curve results from short-term debt instruments having a lower yield than long-term debt instruments of the same credit quality.

80. D
Pegging is a manipulative trading activity that is designed to prevent the price of a security from falling.

81. A
The Securities Acts Amendments of 1975 gave authority to the Municipal Securities Rulemaking Board (MSRB).

82. B

$B_i = (\rho_{i,m} \times \sigma_i) \div \sigma_m$

$B_i = (0.75 \times 0.144) \div 0.122 = 0.89$

83. D

Stock market anomalies should not occur if markets are fully efficient. They do not support the efficient market hypothesis.

84. C

Qualified dividends are taxed at the long-term capital gains tax rate.

85. D

A nonexempt unregistered security may be sold through a private placement.

86. B

ADRs allow for the trading of international securities in domestic countries. They trade throughout the day, and their dividends are declared in local currencies and paid in U.S. dollars. ADR holders receive foreign tax credits for income tax paid to a foreign country.

87. D

A mutual fund prospectus includes fees and expenses, investment objectives, and principal risks of investing in the fund.

88. A

GNP = GDP + Net income inflow from abroad – Net income outflow to foreign countries

89. A

Brady bonds are dollar-denominated bonds issued by emerging markets (typically Latin American countries) and collateralized by U.S. Treasuries.

90. D

According to the "brochure rule," investment advisers must deliver the brochure to clients not less than 48 hours prior to entering into any written or oral investment advisory contract, or no later than the time of entering into such contract if the client has the right to terminate the contract without penalty within 5 business days after entering into the contract.

91. A

A C Corp is subject to double taxation. Earnings are taxed once at the entity level and again at the individual level once distributions have occurred.

92. D

Under the provisions of ERISA, a fiduciary is an individual that has discretionary authority or responsibility over retirement plan administration, exercises discretionary authority over retirement plan management, renders investment advice for a fee or other compensation, or exercises authority or control over the disposition of retirement plan assets.

93. C

The NASDAQ Composite, Russell 2000, S&P 500, and Wilshire 5000 are value-weighted indexes.

94. D
The standard expiration period for a put or call option is 9 months. Long-term equity anticipation securities (LEAPS) have an expiration period longer than 1 year.

95. A
Incentive stock options (ISOs) may be granted to employees only.

96. C
In a fixed exchange rate system, a country ties its currency to a basket of other currencies or to another measure of value, such as gold.

97. D
Monetary policy is carried out through open market operations, changing the discount rate, and changing the reserve requirements.

98. B
Cash flow from operations = Net income + Depreciation – Increase in accounts receivable + Increase in accounts payable
Cash flow from operations = $660,000 + $35,000 – $110,000 + $120,000 = $705,000

99. D
Securities and Exchange Commission v. W. J. Howey Co. defined an investment contract as "a contract, transaction, or scheme whereby a person invests his money in a common enterprise and is led to expect profits solely from the efforts of the promoter or a third party." The case led to the "Howey test."

100. B
By selling a naked call, the investor is expecting Omikron's stock price to decrease. If the stock increases in value, the investor's potential loss is unlimited.

101. B
Sharpe ratio = $(R_p - R_f) \div S_p$
$0.76 = (R_p - 3.5) \div 9$
$R_p = 10.34\%$

102. B
A regulated investment company passes capital gains, dividends, and interest earned on fund investments directly to shareholders so that it is taxed only at the personal level, and double taxation is avoided.

103. C
A fidelity bond is a form of insurance protection that covers public consumers for losses that they incur as a result of fraudulent acts by specified individuals, such as employees of a broker-dealer.

104. D
The purchase date (January 3rd) is within thirty days of the sale date (December 18th), and is considered a wash sale. This means that no loss deduction is allowed. The amount of the disallowed loss will be added to the cost basis of the shares that Joel purchased on January 3rd.

105. D
For the substantially equal periodic payment (SEPP) exception to the premature distribution penalty, the IRS does not require a reason for taking withdrawals.

106. B
After-tax return $= 0.18 \times (1 - 0.28) = 12.96\%$

107. D
Security D is the answer by process of elimination. Begin with the securities with a beta of 0.8 and select the one with the highest return. This eliminates security A. Next, compare the securities that have an investment return of 6%, and select the one with the least risk (lowest beta). This eliminates security B. Finally, compare the two securities that remain, C and D. Security D provides a higher return for less risk than security C. Therefore, security D is the investment a rational investor would select.

108. D
Stagflation is the result of persistent high inflation combined with high unemployment and a slowing demand for goods and services.

109. D
For a profit sharing plan, contributions may be skewed to favor older participants through methods such as age-weighting and cross-testing. The allocation formula cannot be discriminatory.

110. A
The Alpha and Treynor ratios assume a diversified portfolio. The Sharpe ratio assumes a non-diversified portfolio.

111. C
The two broad categories of defined contribution plans are profit sharing plans and pension plans.

112. C
Unlike a 529 plan, funds in a UGMA/UTMA account do not grow tax-deferred. However, the funds in the UGMA/UTMA account do not need to be used to pay for education expenses. The custodian, typically the minor's parent, does not own the assets in the account. Once the account is set up, it's considered to be an irrevocable gift.

113. A
According to SEC Rule 506(b), private placements may be sold to an unlimited number of accredited investors and up to 35 non-accredited investors.

114. B
There is a 10% penalty on premature distributions from a qualified plan, 403(b) plan, IRA, or SEP.

115. B
As bond interest rates decrease, bond duration increases.

116. A

2 quarters – 1 quarter = 1 quarter

An economic recession is defined as a decline in real GDP for 2 or more consecutive quarters.

117. C

Secured bonds have a legal claim to specific assets in the event of default, insolvency, or liquidation.

118. A

Inferior goods decrease in demand as consumer income increases.

119. A

A pre-emptive right is also referred to as a "subscription right" or a "subscription privilege." It is a right, but not an obligation for existing shareholders to exercise, and it prevents dilution among existing shareholders.

120. B

Hybrid REITs combine features of equity REITs and mortgage REITs.

121. A

Consolidated tape refers to the high-speed electronic system that reports the latest price and volume data on sales of exchange-listed stocks.

122. B

Quick ratio = (Cash + Short-term marketable securities + Receivables) ÷ Current liabilities

Quick ratio = ($150,000 + $90,000 + $195,000) ÷ $200,000 = 2.18

123. C

Cash ratio = (Cash + Short-term marketable securities) ÷ Current liabilities

Cash ratio = ($150,000 + $90,000) ÷ $200,000 = 1.20

124. D

Being a "solicitor" typically involves soliciting, referring, offering, or negotiating the sale of investment advisory services on behalf of a third party financial adviser for monetary compensation. Both individuals and entities can be considered solicitors, and according to SEC Rule 206(4)-3, the terms of the fee to be paid and solicitor activity being conducted must be documented by a written agreement. Individuals that will solicit on behalf of an RIA firm are often required to not only qualify as an individual IAR, but to also establish his or her own investment advisory firm.

125. B

The Trust Indenture Act of 1939 applies to debt securities, such as bonds, debentures, and notes that are offered for public sale. Even though such securities may be registered under the Securities Act, they may not be offered for sale to the public unless a formal agreement between the issuer of bonds and the bondholder conforms to the standards of this act.

126. B
$275,000 \times 15\% = \$41,250$
The maximum contribution is limited by the annual compensation limit for 2018, which is $275,000.

127. D
Regarding municipal bonds, a good faith deposit is the small amount of money, usually less than 5% of an issue, that underwriters give to the issuer in exchange for the right to place part of the issue.

128. D
A fixed income security may be subject to all of the risks listed. This includes systematic risks that are always present (exchange rate risk, purchasing power risk, reinvestment risk), as well as non-systematic risks, such as default risk and liquidity risk.

129. D
The fourth market refers to direct institution-to-institution trading, usually done in blocks, without using the service of broker-dealers.

130. C
The Insider Trading and Securities Fraud Enforcement Act of 1988 established the policies and procedures commonly referred to as a "Chinese wall."

PRACTICE EXAM 3

QUESTIONS

1. Monetary policy refers to actions taken by the _____ to control the money supply, often by targeting a specific rate of interest.

   A. Executive branch
   B. FDIC
   C. Federal Reserve
   D. U.S. Treasury

2. On a company's balance sheet, liabilities are reported at their:

   A. beginning of year balance.
   B. current outstanding balance.
   C. end of year balance.
   D. initial loan amount.

3. All but which of the following are correct regarding Treasury notes?

   A. They are issued by the U.S. Treasury Department.
   B. They have maturities of 10 years or less.
   C. They make variable interest payments on a semiannual basis.
   D. They are taxed at the federal level only.

4. Which of the following determines if a security being considered for inclusion in an investor's portfolio offers an adequate expected return for the level of risk assumed?

   A. Capital market line
   B. Security market line
   C. Support line
   D. Trendline

5. Which of the following is the correct method to conducting top-down investment analysis?

   A. First examine a specific company, then examine a specific industry, then examine a specific economy, then examine the global economy.
   B. First examine a specific company, then examine a specific economy, then examine a specific industry, then examine the global economy.
   C. First examine the global economy, then examine a specific industry, then examine a specific economy, then examine a specific company.
   D. First examine the global economy, then examine a specific economy, then examine a specific industry, then examine a specific company.

6. Which of the following investment strategies are profitable in a rising stock market?

   (1) Buying a call
   (2) Buying a put
   (3) Selling a put
   (4) Selling a call

   A. (1) and (3) only
   B. (1) and (4) only
   C. (2) and (3) only
   D. (2) and (4) only

7. Which of the following acts established a non-profit membership corporation that over-sees the liquidation of member broker-dealers that close when the broker-dealer is bankrupt or in financial trouble, and customer assets are missing?

   A. Securities Investor Protection Corporation Act of 1970
   B. Securities Act Amendments of 1975
   C. Uniform Prudent Investors Act of 1994
   D. National Securities Market Improvement Act of 1996

8. An RIA firm must typically register or notice file in a state when it has more than _____ clients who are located in that state.

   A. 5
   B. 10
   C. 15
   D. 20

9. Client information must be kept confidential unless which of the following circumstances apply?

   A. The information is needed to establish an advisory or brokerage account.
   B. The information is required in response to proper legal process.
   C. The information is in connection with a civil dispute between the adviser and the client.
   D. All of the above are correct.

10. The Dow Jones Industrial Average is a/an _____ average of _____ blue chip U.S. stocks.

   A. equal-weighted, 30
   B. equal-weighted, 500
   C. price-weighted, 30
   D. price-weighted, 500

11. Which of the following are correct regarding credits and deductions?

    (1) A deduction is more beneficial to a lower-bracket taxpayer.
    (2) A deduction is more beneficial to a higher-bracket taxpayer.
    (3) A credit is more beneficial to a lower-bracket taxpayer.
    (4) A credit is more beneficial to a higher-bracket taxpayer.

    A. (1) and (3) only
    B. (1) and (4) only
    C. (2) and (3) only
    D. (2) and (4) only

12. Which of the following is a type of revocable trust in which the corpus consists of bank accounts and/or bank assets? At the grantor's death, the trust becomes irrevocable and avoids probate.

    A. Marital trust
    B. Payable on death trust
    C. Totten trust
    D. Transfer on death trust

13. Which of the following is an electronic filing system that facilitates investment adviser registration, exempt reporting adviser filing, regulatory review, and the public disclosure information of registered investment adviser firms and individuals?

    A. ADV
    B. CRD
    C. EDGAR
    D. IARD

14. American Depository Receipts (ADRs) have which of the following characteristics?

    (1) Dividends paid from an ADR are first declared in the local currency.
    (2) American Depository Receipts eliminate exchange rate risk.

    A. (1) only
    B. (2) only
    C. Both (1) and (2) are correct.
    D. Neither (1) or (2) are correct.

15. A/An _____ legal opinion indicates that a bond counsel has concerns regarding one or more of the statements in the bond issue.

    A. binding
    B. enforceable
    C. qualified
    D. unqualified

16. Which of the following is considered an indicator of market volatility based on the premiums that investors are willing to pay for the right to buy or sell a stock?

   A. AGG
   B. IWD
   C. SPY
   D. VIX

17. Which of the following is/are correct regarding capital losses?

   (1) Capital losses have a two-year carry back period.
   (2) Capital losses have a five-year carry forward period.

   A. (1) only
   B. (2) only
   C. Both (1) and (2) are correct.
   D. Neither (1) or (2) are correct.

18. All but which of the following are characteristics of a SEP IRA?

   A. It is entirely owned by the participant.
   B. Plan loans are permitted.
   C. The contribution deadline to a SEP IRA is April 15, including extensions.
   D. The account balance is 100% vested at all times.

19. A loss on the sale of securities is not deductible if a taxpayer purchases identical securities within _____ prior to or after the date of sale.

   A. 7 days
   B. 14 days
   C. 30 days
   D. 60 days

20. Which of the following are correct regarding incentive stock options (ISOs) and non-qualified stock options (NQSOs)?

   (1) Unlike an ISO, an NQSO does not have to meet any specific holding period rules.
   (2) Unlike an NQSO, an ISO does not have to meet any specific holding period rules.
   (3) With an ISO, the employee incurs a taxable event at the time the option is exercised.
   (4) With an NQSO, the employee incurs a taxable event at the time the option is exercised.

   A. (1) and (3) only
   B. (1) and (4) only
   C. (2) and (3) only
   D. (1), (3), and (4) only

21. Which of the following is the formula to calculate an investment's taxable equivalent yield?

    A. Taxable equivalent yield = Tax-free yield ÷ (1 – Marginal tax rate)
    B. Taxable equivalent yield = Tax-free yield ÷ (1 + Marginal tax rate)
    C. Taxable equivalent yield = (1 – Marginal tax rate) ÷ Tax-free yield
    D. Taxable equivalent yield = (1 + Marginal tax rate) ÷ Tax-free yield

22. Which of the following is/are correct regarding a bond's interest rate and term to maturity?

    (1) The lower a bond's interest rate, the lower its relative price fluctuation.
    (2) The longer a bond's term to maturity, the greater its relative price fluctuation.

    A. (1) only
    B. (2) only
    C. Both (1) and (2) are correct.
    D. Neither (1) or (2) are correct.

For questions 23 – 25, match the economic policy with the description that follows. Use only one answer per blank. Answers may be used more than once or not at all.

    A. Expansionary policy
    B. Contractionary policy

23. ___ Taxes increase

24. ___ Public spending increases

25. ___ Government borrowing decreases

26. Investment advisers must amend Form ADV each year by filing an annual updating amendment within how many days of the end of their fiscal year?

    A. 30 days
    B. 60 days
    C. 90 days
    D. 120 days

27. In a long call, the maximum gain is _____ and the maximum loss is _____.

    A. limited, unlimited
    B. the premium paid, unlimited
    C. unlimited, the premium paid
    D. unlimited, unlimited

28. Which of the following is/are correct regarding the objectives of ERISA?

    (1) ERISA establishes criteria for investment selection for qualified retirement plans.
    (2) ERISA establishes minimum funding, eligibility, coverage, and vesting require-
        ments for qualified retirement plans.

    A. (1) only
    B. (2) only
    C. Both (1) and (2) are correct.
    D. Neither (1) or (2) are correct.

29. Which of the following is correct regarding a bond's coupon rate?

    A. It is the stated annual interest rate that will be paid each period for the term of a
       bond.
    B. It is stated as a percentage of the current market price of a bond.
    C. A 5% coupon bond will pay $50 each semiannual period for a $1,000 bond.
    D. A bond's coupon rate is also its yield to maturity (YTM).

30. In which of the following trusts is the surviving spouse given a general power of ap-
    pointment by the decedent spouse to distribute the decedent's property as the surviv-
    ing spouse determines? Since the surviving spouse holds a general power of appoint-
    ment, he or she may use trust assets to benefit him or herself directly.

    A. Credit shelter trust
    B. Estate trust
    C. Marital trust
    D. QTIP trust

31. Which of the following acts transferred the responsibility for rulemaking and enforce-
    ment of identity theft Red Flags Rules to the SEC and CFTC for the firms they regulate?

    A. Insider Trading and Securities Fraud Enforcement Act of 1988
    B. Patriot Act of 2001
    C. Sarbanes-Oxley Act of 2002
    D. Dodd-Frank Wall Street Reform and Consumer Protection Act of 2010

32. Interest earned from Series EE bonds may be excluded from gross income if the pro-
    ceeds are used to pay for which of the following?

    A. First-time home purchase.
    B. Medical expenses exceeding 7.5% of income.
    C. Qualified higher education expenses.
    D. Tax bill owed to the IRS.

33. Which of the following are insurance industry rating services?

(1) A.M. Best
(2) Fitch
(3) NAIC
(4) Standard & Poor's

A. (1) and (2) only
B. (1), (2), and (4) only
C. (2), (3), and (4) only
D. All of the above are correct.

34. Theta LLC provides the following information on their year-end financial statement:

Common stock	$205,000
Retained earnings	$230,000
Long-term debt	$615,000
Effective tax rate	35%

What is Theta LLC's debt-to-capital ratio?

A. 0.59
B. 0.73
C. 0.75
D. 0.77

35. Which of the following is a group of underwriters who agree to purchase the shares of an IPO from an issuer and then sell the shares to investors?

A. Registered investment advisers
B. Regulated investment company
C. Solicitors
D. Syndicate

For questions 36 – 39, match the type of risk with the description that follows. Use only one answer per blank. Answers may be used more than once or not at all.

A. Systematic risk
B. Unsystematic risk

36. ___ Default risk

37. ___ Political risk

38. ___ Reinvestment risk

39. ___ Tax risk

40. Which of the following is correct regarding defensive stocks?

    A. They are stocks that invest in the defense sector of the U.S. economy.
    B. They are stocks that are unaffected by general fluctuations in the economy.
    C. They are stocks that are tax efficient and therefore "defensive" for tax purposes.
    D. They are stocks that are unaffected by changes in interest rates.

41. Which of the following is correct regarding the relationship between a bond's coupon and its duration?

    A. Higher coupon = Lower duration = Lower interest rate risk
    B. Higher coupon = Higher duration = Higher interest rate risk
    C. Higher coupon = Lower duration = Higher interest rate risk
    D. Higher coupon = Higher duration = Lower interest rate risk

The following information relates to questions 42 – 43.

Alpha Corporation provides the following information for the fiscal year (in millions):

Revenue	$51.5
Cost of goods sold	$29.0
Other operating expenses	$6.5
Interest expense	$1.1
Tax expense	$1.6
Effective tax rate	28%

42. What is Alpha Corporation's gross profit?

    A. $6.5 million
    B. $13.3 million
    C. $22.5 million
    D. $23.6 million

43. What is Alpha Corporation's net income?

    A. $6.5 million
    B. $13.3 million
    C. $22.5 million
    D. $23.6 million

44. All but which of the following are considered securities under the Uniform Securities Act?

    A. Debentures
    B. Precious metals
    C. Variable annuities
    D. Variable life insurance

45. Which of the following is a type of debt issued by a national government in a foreign currency in order to finance the issuing country's growth and development?

   A. Domestic debt
   B. Eurodebt
   C. Foreign debt
   D. Sovereign debt

46. Which of the following is true regarding gift splitting?

   A. A married couple can select which gifts made during the year will receive split gift treatment.
   B. A gift made after one spouse dies can still be split.
   C. The split gift election is commonly used with community property.
   D. When the gift splitting election is made, gifts made by either spouse are treated as being made one-half by each spouse.

47. Which of the following is the FINRA committee that reviews initial decisions rendered in FINRA disciplinary and membership proceedings? It may affirm, dismiss, modify, or reverse any finding, or remand the case for further proceedings.

   A. Board of Governors
   B. FINRA Disciplinary Council
   C. National Adjudicatory Council
   D. None of the above are correct.

48. Assume that Zeta stock pays a constant dividend of $4.10 per share each year. The dividend is not expected to grow. If an investor has a required rate of return of 7%, what is the value of Zeta stock?

   A. $4.39 per share
   B. $17.07 per share
   C. $58.57 per share
   D. $69.10 per share

49. Mary has taxable income of $200,000 and a tax liability of $55,000. Mike has taxable income of $150,000 and a tax liability of $35,000. Which of the following tax rate structures is being used to tax Mary and Mike?

   A. Flat
   B. Progressive
   C. Regressive
   D. Value added

50. Thomas, age 53, recently quit his job. He would like to distribute money from his 401(k) but wants to avoid any penalties related to the distribution. If he waits a minimum of _____ years, his distribution will not be subject to the _____ premature distribution penalty.

    A. 2, 10%
    B. 2, 15%
    C. 6, 15%
    D. 6, 20%

51. Which of the following is a self-regulatory organization (SRO)?

    A. FINRA
    B. NYSE
    C. SIPC
    D. All of the above are correct.

52. Which of the following is/are correct regarding a qualified personal residence trust (QPRT)?

    (1) A QPRT is generally appropriate for vacation homes valued over $1 million.
    (2) A QPRT is ideal for a single parent in his or her 30s or 40s.
    (3) The grantor will have a taxable gift upon the creation of a QPRT.
    (4) After the trust term ends, the house reverts back to the grantor.

    A. (1) only
    B. (1) and (3) only
    C. (2) and (4) only
    D. (1), (3), and (4) only

53. All but which of the following are correct regarding Treasury bills?

    A. They have maturities of one year or less.
    B. They are sold in minimum denominations of $500.
    C. They are considered to be risk free of default.
    D. They are sold at a discount to par.

54. Which of the following accurately describes the difference between rights and warrants?

    (1) A warrant may be attached to new debt or preferred issues to make the issues more attractive to buyers.
    (2) Rights and warrants have different lifespans.
    (3) Warrants usually expire within a few weeks.
    (4) Rights may continue without expiring for up to several years.

    A. (1) only
    B. (1) and (2) only
    C. (2), (3), and (4) only
    D. All of the above are correct.

55. Which of the following was the self-regulatory organization for the over-the-counter market, and is now part of FINRA?

A. NAC
B. NASAA
C. NASD
D. NYSE

56. Which of the following will increase an employer's contribution to a defined benefit plan?

(1) Lower than expected investment returns
(2) High turnover among employees
(3) High ratio of married to unmarried participants
(4) Large forfeitures

A. (1) and (2) only
B. (1) and (3) only
C. (2) and (3) only
D. (3) and (4) only

57. Which of the following yield curves results from similar yields among Treasury notes, Treasury bonds, and Treasury bills?

A. Flat yield curve
B. Inverted yield curve
C. Negative yield curve
D. Steep yield curve

58. Common stock is referred to as _____ because the owner of the stock is also an owner of the corporation and may participate in its capital and income growth.

A. cumulative stock
B. debt
C. equity
D. preferred stock

59. Which of the following is/are correct regarding closed-end mutual funds?

(1) Closed-end mutual funds may issue new shares when an individual buys existing shares.
(2) Closed-end mutual funds may sell at a premium or discount to their net asset value.

A. (1) only
B. (2) only
C. Both (1) and (2) are correct.
D. Neither (1) or (2) are correct.

60. Which of the following is the correct reason to purchase a particular investment for a client's portfolio?

A. Growth stocks because they pay high dividends.
B. FNMA securities because they are backed by the full faith and credit of the U.S. government.
C. Global fund because it provides only international exposure.
D. Blue chip common stocks because they provide a hedge against inflation.

61. According to the Telephone Consumer Protection Act, solicitors are prohibited from calling residences before _____ and after _____ local time.

A. 7 a.m., 10 p.m.
B. 8 a.m., 9 p.m.
C. 9 a.m., 5 p.m.
D. 10 a.m., 8 p.m.

62. Which of the following accounts is most suitable to hold a zero-coupon bond?

A. IRA
B. Joint taxable account
C. Payable on death account
D. Totten trust

63. How is the original basis of a newly acquired asset calculated? Assume the asset was acquired at an arm's length transaction from a non-related party.

A. Cost minus expenses of sale, such as sales tax paid, installation costs, freight charges, and commissions incurred in acquiring the asset.
B. Cost plus expenses of sale, such as sales tax paid, installation costs, freight charges, and commissions incurred in acquiring the asset.
C. Cost plus commissions incurred in acquiring the asset only.
D. Cost minus commissions incurred in acquiring the asset only.

64. All but which of the following are characteristics of an employee stock purchase plan (ESPP)?

A. The plan must be offered to employees on a nondiscriminatory basis.
B. The maximum discount permitted is 15% of the greater of the market price on the date the option is granted or the date the shares were purchased.
C. The maximum fair market value of stock that an employee has the right to purchase cannot exceed $100,000 in any calendar year.
D. An ESPP allows a company to sell stock to employees at a discount from the market price.

65. Current assets ÷ Current liabilities = _____

    A. Current ratio
    B. Debt-to-equity ratio
    C. Quick ratio
    D. Return on assets

66. All but which of the following are correct regarding investment adviser representatives (IARs)?

    A. Every investment advisory firm must have at least one IAR registered to the firm.
    B. An IAR can be a dual registrant of multiple firms in some states only.
    C. There are currently no continuing education requirements for IARs.
    D. An IAR does not need to be registered to an RIA firm in order to conduct investment advisory business.

67. The holding period of inherited property is considered to be _____ in nature.

    A. always short-term
    B. always long-term
    C. sometimes short-term
    D. sometimes long-term

The following information relates to questions 68 – 70.

A convertible bond is issued with a par value of $10,000. The bond is currently priced at $9,500, and the underlying share price is $200.

68. The conversion ratio of the bond is:

    A. 47.5:1.
    B. 50.0:1.
    C. 52.5:1.
    D. 55.5:1.

69. The conversion value of the bond is:

    A. $9,500.
    B. $9,700.
    C. $9,800.
    D. $10,000.

70. The conversion condition for the bond is:

    A. below parity.
    B. at parity.
    C. above parity.
    D. unknown.

71. Which of the following determines the minimum margin requirement for investment accounts?

    A. Congress
    B. FDIC
    C. Federal Reserve
    D. SIPC

72. An investor purchased a share of Kappa stock for $184 and sold it for $173. If a $4.25 dividend was paid during the holding period, what was the total return?

    A. –4.67%
    B. –4.33%
    C. –4.02%
    D. –3.67%

For questions 73 – 77, determine how basis is treated at death for the following forms of property ownership. Use only one answer per blank. Answers may be used more than once or not at all.

    A. Step-up in basis for one-half property.
    B. Full step-up in basis to the extent the property is included in the decedent's gross estate.
    C. Full step-up in basis.

73. ___ Joint tenants with rights of survivorship between spouses

74. ___ Joint tenants with rights of survivorship between non-spouses

75. ___ Tenancy by entirety

76. ___ Tenancy in common

77. ___ Community property

78. All but which of the following are correct regarding Series I bonds?

    A. They are adjusted for inflation as measured by the Consumer Price Index.
    B. They are taxed at the state level only.
    C. They are guaranteed to never lose value, even during deflationary periods.
    D. They are non-marketable bonds that cannot be bought or sold in the secondary market.

79. Which of the following groups may be eligible to participate in a 403(b) plan?

    A. Church employees
    B. Not-for-profit hospital employees
    C. Public school employees
    D. All of the above are correct.

80. According to _____, when an issuer discloses material nonpublic information to certain individuals or entities, typically securities market professionals, the issuer must make public disclosure of that information, as well.

    A. Regulation BB
    B. Regulation CF
    C. Regulation FD
    D. Regulation SK

81. Which of the following describes the relationship between total risk, systematic risk, and unsystematic risk?

    A. Total risk = Systematic risk – Unsystematic risk
    B. Total risk – Systematic risk = Unsystematic risk
    C. Total risk + Unsystematic risk = Systematic risk
    D. Unsystematic risk – Total risk = Systematic risk

For questions 82 – 86, match the term with the description that follows. Use only one answer per blank. Answers may be used more than once or not at all.

    A. Call loan rate
    B. Discount rate
    C. Fed funds rate
    D. LIBOR
    E. Prime rate

82. ___ The minimum interest rate set by the Federal Reserve for lending to other banks.

83. ___ The interest rate at which depository institutions (banks and credit unions) lend reserve balances to other depository institutions overnight, on a collateralized basis.

84. ___ The short-term interest rate charged by banks on loans extended to broker-dealers, who then use the funds to make margin loans on behalf of customers.

85. ___ The interest rate that banks charge their most credit-worthy customers, typically large corporations.

86. ___ The benchmark rate that international banks charge each other for short-term loans.

87. Which of the following lists the stages of money laundering in the correct order?

    A. Layering, integration, placement
    B. Layering, placement, integration
    C. Placement, integration, layering
    D. Placement, layering, integration

88. Information such as fee schedule, services offered, key advisory personnel, conflicts of interest, and educational background are typically included in the:

A. ADV.
B. CRD.
C. IARD.
D. U4.

89. Which of the following is a value-weighted index measuring the overall performance of the U.S. stock market?

A. Dow Jones Industrial Average
B. EAFE Index
C. Russell 2000
D. Wilshire 5000

90. Epsilon stock has an expected return of 7.2% and a beta of 0.95. If the risk-free rate is 2.5%, then the expected return for the market, according to the capital asset pricing model, is:

A. 6.84%.
B. 7.45%.
C. 7.96%.
D. 8.02%.

91. For the substantially equal periodic payment (SEPP) exception to apply for premature distributions from a retirement plan, payments must continue for _____ or until the participant is _____, whichever is longer.

A. 5 years, age 59 ½
B. 5 years, age 65
C. 10 years, age 59 ½
D. 10 years, age 65

92. Which of the following provides clearing, settlement, risk management, central counterparty services, and a guarantee of completion for certain transactions for virtually all broker-to-broker trades involving equities, corporate and municipal debt, ADRs, ETFs, and UITs?

A. ATC
B. NSCC
C. OCC
D. TRACE

93. A mutual fund with a high turnover rate will require _____ active management and will typically charge _____ expenses.

A. less, higher
B. less, lower
C. more, higher
D. more, lower

94. All but which of the following are correct regarding probate?

A. It provides for clean title to a decedent's property.
B. It's the process by which a state or local court validates a decedent's will.
C. It protects the decedent from an untimely filing of claims by his or her lifetime creditors.
D. It may be either a public or private process depending on the wishes of the decedent.

95. Monica, age 60, is listed as beneficiary of her brother's $350,000 life insurance policy. She is single and pays 20% federal taxes and 10% state taxes. If Monica's brother were to die, how much tax would she owe?

A. $0
B. $35,000
C. $70,000
D. $105,000

96. Which of the following is correct regarding the selling price of Treasury STRIPS?

A. They are sold at a discount from face value.
B. They are sold at a premium to face value.
C. They are sold at face value.
D. They are sold at either a discount or premium to face value.

97. All but which of the following are correct regarding Electronic Communication Networks (ECNs)?

A. They are a type of alternative trading system (ATS).
B. They trade unlisted stocks and other non-exchange-traded products.
C. Unlike dark pools, ECNs display orders in the consolidated quote stream.
D. ECNs are required to register with the SEC as broker-dealers.

98. The typical grace period for a life insurance policy is:

A. 7 days.
B. 14 days.
C. 30 days.
D. 60 days.

99. The standard deviation of an investment portfolio must be _____ the weighted average of the standard deviation of returns of the individual securities.

   A. equal to
   B. greater than
   C. less than
   D. less than or equal to

100. To establish a Coverdell Education Savings Account (ESA), the beneficiary must be under age _____ unless the individual is designated as a special needs beneficiary.

   A. 14
   B. 18
   C. 21
   D. 30

101. Which of the following is a fee deducted from a mutual fund's assets to pay for marketing and distribution costs associated with operating the fund?

   A. Accounting fee
   B. Custodial fee
   C. Transfer agent fee
   D. 12b-1 fee

102. Which of the following type of bond is unregistered, with no record kept regarding the owner or transactions involving ownership?

   A. Bearer bond
   B. Brady bond
   C. Fidelity bond
   D. Surety bond

103. According to FINRA, which of the following elements must be addressed in a firm's business continuity plan relating to an emergency or significant business disruption?

   A. Alternate physical location of employees
   B. Communications with regulators
   C. Data backup and recovery
   D. All of the above are correct.

104. An investor deposited $150 in an interest-bearing account earning 6% annually. Assuming the interest is not withdrawn, the amount of interest earned in the third year will be:

   A. $9.00.
   B. $9.54.
   C. $10.11.
   D. $10.72.

105. Which of the following acts gives consumers the right to one free credit report each year from the credit reporting agencies? It also allows consumers to purchase, for a reasonable fee, a credit score along with information about how the credit score was calculated.

    A. Securities Act Amendments of 1975
    B. Insider Trading and Securities Fraud Enforcement Act of 1988
    C. FACT Act of 2003
    D. Dodd-Frank Wall Street Reform and Consumer Protection Act of 2010

106. Kappa Fund has a Treynor ratio of 4.71. If the fund's return is 11%, and the risk-free rate is 2%, what is the fund's beta?

    A. 1.75
    B. 1.86
    C. 1.88
    D. 1.91

107. Which of the following is a manipulative trading activity that is designed to prevent the price of a security from rising?

    A. Capping
    B. Front running
    C. Painting the tape
    D. Pegging

108. Which of the following are basic provisions of a universal life insurance policy?

    (1) Flexible death benefit
    (2) Flexible premium
    (3) Minimum guaranteed cash value
    (4) Unbundled structure

    A. (1) and (2) only
    B. (2) and (3) only
    C. (1), (2), and (4) only
    D. (1), (3), and (4) only

109. Assume that an investor wants to dollar cost average into Delta mutual fund by making quarterly purchases over a two-year period. If the total amount to be invested is $48,000, then how much will be invested each quarter if the fund's NAV increases by a total of 10% over the two-year period?

    A. $6,000
    B. $6,600
    C. $8,000
    D. $8,800

110. SEC-registered advisers are not required to deliver a brochure to clients who receive only impersonal investment advice from the adviser and who will pay the adviser less than _____ per year.

A. $100
B. $500
C. $1,000
D. $1,500

111. Which of the following models determines the intrinsic value of a stock based on future dividends that grow at a non-changing rate?

A. Adjustable dividend growth model
B. CAPM dividend growth model
C. Constant dividend growth model
D. Intrinsic dividend growth model

112. A health savings account (HSA) allows the account holder to set aside money on a/an _____ basis to pay for _____ medical expenses.

A. after-tax, qualified
B. after-tax, unqualified
C. pre-tax, qualified
D. pre-tax, unqualified

113. Which of the following refers to a computerized system used by the NYSE to display, record, and execute orders for securities?

A. Automated quotation system
B. Order management system
C. Super display book system
D. None of the above are correct.

114. An investor purchased a share of Omikron stock for $90.00 and sold it for $95.50. If the total return was 7.50%, the dividend paid during the holding period was:

A. $1.20.
B. $1.25.
C. $1.35.
D. $1.40.

115. Which of the following is an order to sell a security at or above a specified price?

A. Sell limit order
B. Sell market order
C. Sell top order
D. None of the above are correct.

116. Which of the following preserves and promotes public confidence in the U.S. financial system by insuring deposits in banks by identifying, monitoring, and addressing risks to the deposit insurance funds; and by limiting the effect on the economy when a financial institution fails?

    A. FDIC
    B. NASD
    C. PBGC
    D. SIPC

117. Phil has owned his company, Beta Corporation, for 15 years. He is now 52 years old and plans to retire at age 64. He has five young employees and wants to establish a retirement plan that will provide him with the highest benefit. Assuming adequate cash flow, which of the following is the most suitable plan for Beta Corporation to establish?

    A. Age-based profit sharing plan
    B. Defined benefit plan
    C. Money purchase plan
    D. SIMPLE IRA

118. Which of the following is a type of debt security that repackages and directs the payments of principal and interest from a collateral pool to different types and maturities of securities?

    A. CMO
    B. GIC
    C. REIT
    D. UIT

119. All companies, foreign and domestic, are required to file registration statements, periodic reports, and other forms electronically through which of the following? Consumers can then access and download this information for free.

    A. CRD
    B. EDGAR
    C. IARD
    D. NSCC

120. Which of the following is/are correct regarding loan provisions in a SIMPLE plan?

    (1) Loans from a SIMPLE IRA are not permitted.
    (2) Loans from a SIMPLE 401(k) plan are permitted.

    A. (1) only
    B. (2) only
    C. Both (1) and (2) are correct.
    D. Neither (1) or (2) are correct.

121. To be considered a "qualified purchaser," an individual must have not less than _____ in investments.

    A. $1 million
    B. $2 million
    C. $5 million
    D. $10 million

122. Which of the following is a type of debt that allows the lender to collect from the debtor and the debtor's assets in the case of default, as opposed to foreclosing on a particular property or asset?

    A. Nonrecourse loan
    B. Private annuity
    C. Recourse loan
    D. Self-cancelling installment note

For questions 123 – 125, select the relationship that best describes the bond characteristics provided. Use only one answer per blank. Answers may be used more than once or not at all.

    A. Inverse relationship
    B. Direct relationship

123. ___ The coupon rate of a bond and its duration.

124. ___ The maturity date of a bond and its duration.

125. ___ The yield to maturity of a bond and its duration.

126. Which of the following is the voice of state securities agencies responsible for efficient capital formation and grass-roots investor protection in the U.S.? Their fundamental mission is to protect consumers who purchase securities or investment advice, and their jurisdiction extends to a wide variety of issuers and intermediaries who offer and sell securities to the public.

    A. NAIC
    B. NASAA
    C. NASD
    D. SIPC

127. All but which of the following are correct regarding unit investment trusts (UITs)?

    A. Units may be bought or sold on the secondary market.
    B. Upon termination of a UIT, any remaining securities in the trust will be sold and proceeds will be paid to investors.
    C. Units are sold to investors for a minimum cost of $100,000.
    D. They typically have low fees and expenses.

128. Which of the following are correct regarding Roth IRAs?

(1) Contributions to a Roth IRA can be made at any age.
(2) Contributions to a Roth IRA must be made before age 70 ½.
(3) A Roth IRA owner is not required to take a minimum distribution during his or her lifetime.
(4) Roth IRA contributions may be deducted in limited circumstances.

A. (1) and (3) only
B. (2) and (3) only
C. (1), (3), and (4) only
D. (2), (3), and (4) only

129. Firms must retain blotters containing all purchases and sales of securities for at least _____ years, and they must keep copies of confirmations for _____ years. For the first _____ years, these records must be kept in an easily accessible location.

A. 3, 2, 2
B. 4, 3, 2
C. 5, 4, 3
D. 6, 3, 2

130. Which of the following is correct regarding the taxation of TIPS?

A. TIPS are taxed at the federal level only.
B. TIPS are taxed at the state level only.
C. TIPS are taxed at the state and federal level.
D. TIPS are tax-free at both the state and federal level.

ANSWER KEY

1. C
Monetary policy refers to actions taken by the Federal Reserve to control the money supply, often by targeting a specific rate of interest.

2. B
On a company's balance sheet, liabilities are reported at their current outstanding balance.

3. C
Treasury notes are issued by the U.S. Treasury Department and have maturities of 10 years or less. They have fixed interest payments that are made semiannually to maturity, and they are taxed at the federal level only.

4. B
The security market line determines if a security being considered for inclusion in an investor's portfolio offers an adequate expected return for the level of risk assumed.

5. D
To conduct top-down investment analysis, first examine the global economy, then examine a specific economy, then examine a specific industry, then examine a specific company.

6. A
Buying a call and selling a put are bullish strategies. Investors choose these options when they expect the stock market to rise.

7. A
The Securities Investor Protection Corporation Act of 1970 established a non-profit membership corporation that oversees the liquidation of member broker-dealers that close when the broker-dealer is bankrupt or in financial trouble, and customer assets are missing.

8. A
An RIA firm must typically register or notice file in a state when it has more than 5 clients who are located in that state.

9. D
Client information must be kept confidential unless the information is needed to establish an advisory or brokerage account, the information is required in response to proper legal process, or the information is in connection with a civil dispute between the adviser and the client.

10. C
The Dow Jones Industrial Average is a price-weighted average of 30 blue chip U.S. stocks.

11. C
A deduction is more beneficial to a higher-bracket taxpayer, and a credit is more beneficial to a lower-bracket taxpayer.

12. C
A Totten trust is a type of revocable trust in which the corpus consists of bank accounts and/or bank assets. At the grantor's death, the trust becomes irrevocable and avoids probate.

13. D
The IARD is an electronic filing system that facilitates investment adviser registration, exempt reporting adviser filing, regulatory review, and the public disclosure information of registered investment adviser firms and individuals.

14. A
Dividends paid from an ADR are first declared in the local currency, so exchange rate risk will exist.

15. C
A qualified legal opinion indicates that a bond counsel has concerns regarding one or more of the statements in the bond issue.

16. D
The VIX is considered an indicator of market volatility based on the premiums that investors are willing to pay for the right to buy or sell a stock.

17. B
Capital losses have a three-year carry back period and a five-year carry forward period.

18. B
A SEP IRA is entirely owned by the participant, and the account balance is 100% vested at all times. The contribution deadline to a SEP IRA is April 15, including extensions. Plan loans are not permitted from a SEP IRA.

19. C
A loss on the sale of securities is not deductible if a taxpayer purchases identical securities within 30 days prior to or after the date of sale. This is referred to as the wash sale rule.

20. B
Unlike an ISO, an NQSO does not have to meet any specific holding period rules. With an NQSO, the employee incurs a taxable event at the time the option is exercised.

21. A
Taxable equivalent yield = Tax-free yield ÷ (1 – Marginal tax rate)

22. B
The lower a bond's interest rate, the greater its relative price fluctuation. The longer a bond's term to maturity, the greater its relative price fluctuation.

23. B

Contractionary policy is characterized by taxes increasing, public spending decreasing, and government borrowing decreasing.

24. A

Expansionary policy is characterized by taxes decreasing, public spending increasing, and government borrowing increasing.

25. B

Contractionary policy is characterized by taxes increasing, public spending decreasing, and government borrowing decreasing.

26. C

Investment advisers must amend Form ADV each year by filing an annual updating amendment within 90 days of the end of their fiscal year.

27. C

In a long call, the maximum gain is unlimited and the maximum loss is the premium paid.

28. B

ERISA establishes minimum funding, eligibility, coverage, and vesting requirements for qualified retirement plans.

29. A

A bond's coupon rate is the stated annual interest rate that will be paid each period for the term of a bond. It is stated as a percentage of the face value of the bond.

30. C

In a marital trust, the surviving spouse is given a general power of appointment by the decedent spouse to distribute the decedent's property as the surviving spouse determines. Since the surviving spouse holds a general power of appointment, he or she may use trust assets to benefit him or herself directly.

31. D

The Dodd-Frank Wall Street Reform and Consumer Protection Act of 2010 transferred the responsibility for rulemaking and enforcement of identity theft Red Flags Rules to the SEC and CFTC for the firms they regulate.

32. C

Interest earned from Series EE bonds may be excluded from gross income if the proceeds are used to pay for qualified higher education expenses.

33. B

The insurance industry rating services listed are A.M. Best, Fitch, and Standard & Poor's. The NAIC is the National Association of Insurance Commissioners, and it is not an industry rating service.

34. A
Debt-to-capital ratio = Total debt ÷ (Total debt + Shareholders' equity)
Debt-to-capital ratio = $615,000 ÷ ($615,000 + $205,000 + $230,000) = 0.59

35. D
A syndicate is a group of underwriters who agree to purchase the shares of an IPO from an issuer and then sell the shares to investors.

36. B
Default risk is a type of unsystematic risk.

37. B
Political risk is a type of unsystematic risk.

38. A
Reinvestment risk is a type of systematic risk.

39. B
Tax risk is a type of unsystematic risk.

40. B
Defensive stocks are unaffected by general fluctuations in the economy. They include food, tobacco, and oil stocks.

41. A
Higher coupon = Lower duration = Lower interest rate risk

42. C
Gross profit = Revenue – Cost of goods sold
Gross profit = $51.5 million – $29.0 million = $22.5 million

43. B
Net income = Revenue – Expenses
Net income = $51.5 million – $29.0 million – $6.5 million – $1.1 million – $1.6 million
Net income = $13.3 million

44. B
Debentures, variable annuities, and variable life insurance are considered securities under the Uniform Securities Act. Precious metals are not considered securities.

45. D
Sovereign debt is issued by a national government in a foreign currency in order to finance the issuing country's growth and development.

46. D
When the gift splitting election is made, gifts made by either spouse are treated as being made one-half by each spouse, and all gifts must be split for that particular year.

47. C
The National Adjudicatory Council (NAC) is the FINRA committee that reviews initial decisions rendered in FINRA disciplinary and membership proceedings. It may affirm, dismiss, modify, or reverse any finding, or remand the case for further proceedings.

48. C
Value of Zeta stock = ($4.10 ÷ 0.07) = $58.57 per share

49. B
A progressive tax rate structure is being used to tax Mary and Mike because the tax rate increases as the taxable income increases.

50. A
55 years – 53 years = 2 years
Distributions from a 401(k) following separation from service after age 55 are not subject to the 10% premature distribution penalty.

51. D
FINRA, NYSE, and SIPC are self-regulatory organizations (SROs).

52. B
A qualified personal residence trust (QPRT) is generally appropriate for vacation homes valued over $1 million. The grantor will have a taxable gift upon the creation of a QPRT.

53. B
Treasury bills are sold at a discount to par and have maturities of one year or less. They are considered to be risk free of default and are sold in minimum denominations of $1,000.

54. B
A warrant may be attached to new debt or preferred issues to make the issues more attractive to buyers. A difference between rights and warrants is their lifespan. Rights usually expire within a few weeks, and warrants may continue without expiring for up to several years.

55. C
The NASD (National Association of Securities Dealers) was the self-regulatory organization for the over-the-counter market and is now part of FINRA.

56. B
An employer's annual contributions to a defined benefit plan will increase when the investment returns are lower than expected. A high ratio of married to unmarried participants will also increase employer contributions because pre-retirement death benefits are required for married participants, but not for unmarried participants. High turnover among employees will reduce employer contributions, especially if it leads to large forfeitures. Large forfeitures will provide more funds to pay benefits, resulting in less employer contributions.

57. A
A flat yield curve results from similar yields among Treasury notes, Treasury bonds, and Treasury bills.

58. C
Common stock is referred to as equity because the owner of the stock is also an owner of the corporation and may participate in its capital and income growth.

59. B
Closed-end mutual funds may sell at a premium or discount to their net asset value. Only open-end mutual funds may issue new shares when an individual buys existing shares.

60. D
Blue chip common stocks provide a hedge against inflation. Growth stocks typically reinvest their earnings back into the company rather than pay dividends to shareholders. GNMA securities, not FNMA, are backed by the U.S. government. Global funds invest in both U.S. and international companies.

61. B
According to the Telephone Consumer Protection Act, solicitors are prohibited from calling residences before 8 a.m. and after 9 p.m. local time.

62. A
Of the choices provided, an IRA is the most suitable account to hold a zero-coupon bond because the interest would be tax-deferred. If a zero-coupon bond were held in a taxable account, then tax would be due on the interest earned each year, even though no interest was paid to the bondholder.

63. B
The original basis of a newly acquired asset is equal to the cost plus expenses of sale, such as sales tax paid, installation costs, freight charges, and commissions incurred in acquiring the asset.

64. C
An employee stock purchase plan (ESPP) allows a company to sell stock to employees at a discount from the market price. The plan must be offered to employees on a nondiscriminatory basis, and the maximum discount permitted is 15% of the greater of the market price on the date the option is granted or the date the shares were purchased. The maximum fair market value of stock that an employee has the right to purchase through an ESPP cannot exceed $25,000 in any calendar year.

65. A
Current assets ÷ Current liabilities = Current ratio

66. D
In order to conduct investment advisory business, an investment adviser representative (IAR) must be registered to an RIA firm, and every investment advisory firm must have at least one IAR. An IAR can be a dual registrant of multiple firms in some states only. There are currently no continuing education requirements for IARs.

67. B
The holding period of inherited property is considered to be always long-term in nature.

68. B
Conversion ratio = Par value ÷ Underlying share price
Conversion ratio = $10,000 ÷ $200 = 50:1

69. D
Conversion value = Underlying share price × Conversion ratio
Conversion value = $200 × 50 = $10,000

70. C
Because the current price of the convertible bond is $9,500, the conversion value is greater than the bond's price, or above parity.

71. C
The Federal Reserve determines the minimum margin requirement for investment accounts.

72. D
$R_t = (P_t - P_{t-1} + D_t) \div P_{t-1}$
$R_t = (\$173 - \$184 + \$4.25) \div \$184 = -0.0367 = -3.67\%$

73. A
Joint tenants with rights of survivorship between spouses: Step-up in basis for one-half property.

74. B
Joint tenants with rights of survivorship between non-spouses: Full step-up in basis to the extent the property is included in the decedent's gross estate.

75. A
Tenancy by entirety: Step-up in basis for one-half property.

76. C
Tenancy in common: Full step-up in basis.

77. C
Community property: Full step-up in basis.

78. B
Series I bonds are adjusted for inflation as measured by the Consumer Price Index, and are guaranteed to never lose value, even during deflationary periods. They are non-marketable bonds that cannot be bought or sold in the secondary market, and they are taxed at the federal level only.

79. D
403(b) plan participants may include church employees, not-for-profit hospital employees, and public school employees.

80. C
According to Regulation FD, when an issuer discloses material nonpublic information to certain individuals or entities, typically securities market professionals, the issuer must make public disclosure of that information, as well.

81. B
Total risk = Systematic risk + Unsystematic risk.
This formula can be rewritten as: Total risk – Systematic risk = Unsystematic risk.

82. B
The discount rate is the minimum interest rate set by the Federal Reserve for lending to other banks.

83. C
The Fed funds rate is the interest rate at which depository institutions (banks and credit unions) lend reserve balances to other depository institutions overnight, on a collateral-ized basis.

84. A
The call loan rate is the short-term interest rate charged by banks on loans extended to broker-dealers, who then use the funds to make margin loans on behalf of customers.

85. E
The prime rate is the interest rate that banks charge their most credit-worthy custom-ers, typically large corporations.

86. D
LIBOR is the benchmark rate that international banks charge each other for short-term loans.

87. D
The stages of money laundering, in the correct order, are placement, layering, integra-tion.

88. A
Information such as fee schedule, services offered, key advisory personnel, conflicts of interest, and educational background are typically included in the ADV.

89. D
The Wilshire 5000 is a value-weighted index measuring the overall performance of the U.S. stock market.

90. B
$E(R_i) = R_f + \beta_i[E(R_m) - R_f]$
$7.2\% = 2.5\% + 0.95[E(R_m) - 2.5\%]$
$E(R_m) = 7.45\%$

91. A
For the substantially equal periodic payment (SEPP) exception to apply for premature distributions from a retirement plan, payments must continue for 5 years or until the par-ticipant is age 59 ½, whichever is longer.

92. B
The NSCC (National Securities Clearing Corporation) provides clearing, settlement, risk management, central counterparty services, and a guarantee of completion for certain transactions for virtually all broker-to-broker trades involving equities, corporate and municipal debt, ADRs, ETFs, and UITs.

93. C
A mutual fund with a high turnover rate will require more active management and will typically charge higher expenses.

94. D
Probate is the process by which a state or local court validates a decedent's will. It provides for clean title to a decedent's property and protects a decedent from an untimely filing of claims by his or her lifetime creditors. Probate is a public process.

95. A
Monica would not owe any tax because the death benefit from a life insurance policy is not taxable income.

96. A
Treasury STRIPS are sold at a discount from face value.

97. B
Electronic Communication Networks (ECNs) are a type of alternative trading system (ATS) that trades listed stocks and other exchange-traded products. Unlike dark pools, ECNs display orders in the consolidated quote stream. ECNs are required to register with the SEC as broker-dealers.

98. C
The typical grace period for a life insurance policy is 30 days.

99. D
The standard deviation of an investment portfolio must be less than or equal to the weighted average of the standard deviation of returns of the individual securities. If the securities in a portfolio are perfectly correlated, then the standard deviation of the portfolio will be equal to the weighted average of the standard deviations of the individual securities within the portfolio. If the securities in a portfolio are not perfectly correlated, then the standard deviation of the portfolio will be less than the weighted average of the standard deviations of the individual securities making up the portfolio. By adding additional securities, the standard deviation of the portfolio can never increase.

100. B
To establish a Coverdell Education Savings Account (ESA), the beneficiary must be under age 18 unless the individual is designated as a special needs beneficiary.

101. D
The 12b-1 fee is deducted from a mutual fund's assets to pay for marketing and distribution costs associated with operating the fund.

102. A
A bearer bond is a type of bond that is unregistered, with no record kept regarding the owner or transactions involving ownership.

103. D
According to FINRA, a firm's business continuity plan must address the following relating to an emergency or significant business disruption: An alternate physical location of employees, communications with regulators, and data backup and recovery.

104. C
Step 1: Year 1 value = $150.00 × 1.06 = $159.00
Step 2: Year 2 value = $159.00 × 1.06 = $168.54
Step 3: Year 3 value = $168.54 × 1.06 = $178.65
Step 4: Interest earned in third year = $178.65 − $168.54 = $10.11

105. C
The FACT Act (Fair and Accurate Credit Transactions Act) gives consumers the right to one free credit report each year from the credit reporting agencies. It also allows consumers to purchase, for a reasonable fee, a credit score along with information about how the credit score was calculated.

106. D
Treynor = $(R_p - R_f) \div \beta_p$
$4.71 = (11\% - 2\%) \div \beta_p$
$\beta_p = 1.91$

107. A
Capping is a manipulative trading activity that is designed to prevent the price of a security from rising.

108. C
Universal life insurance policies have a flexible premium and death benefit, and are said to have an "unbundled structure." They do not have a minimum guaranteed cash value.

109. A
$48,000 ÷ 8 quarters = $6,000 per quarter
With dollar cost averaging, a flat dollar amount is invested each period regardless of the underlying investment's performance.

110. B
SEC-registered advisers are not required to deliver a brochure to clients who receive only impersonal investment advice from the adviser and who will pay the adviser less than $500 per year.

111. C
The constant dividend growth model determines the intrinsic value of a stock based on future dividends that grow at a non-changing rate.

112. C
A health savings account (HSA) allows the account holder to set aside money on a pre-tax basis to pay for qualified medical expenses.

113. C

The super display book system is a computerized system used by the NYSE to display, record, and execute orders for securities.

114. B

$R_t = (P_t - P_{t-1} + D_t) \div P_{t-1}$

$0.075 = (\$95.50 - \$90.00 + D_t) \div \$90.00$

$D_t = \$1.25$

115. A

A sell limit order is an order to sell a security at or above a specified price.

116. A

The FDIC preserves and promotes public confidence in the U.S. financial system by insuring deposits in banks by identifying, monitoring, and addressing risks to the deposit insurance funds; and by limiting the effect on the economy when a financial institution fails.

117. B

The defined benefit plan would provide the greatest benefit to Phil because he has five younger employees, and defined benefit plans favor older owner/employees. Of the other options listed, the age-based profit sharing plan is a valid consideration. However, the question says to assume adequate cash flow in the business. Profit sharing plans would benefit unstable cash flow because contributions must only be substantial and recurring. The best answer is the defined benefit plan.

118. A

A CMO (collateralized mortgage obligation) is a type of debt security that repackages and directs the payments of principal and interest from a collateral pool to different types and maturities of securities.

119. B

All companies, foreign and domestic, are required to file registration statements, periodic reports, and other forms electronically through EDGAR (Electronic Data Gathering, Analysis, and Retrieval). Consumers can then access and download this information for free.

120. C

Loans from a SIMPLE IRA are not permitted, but loans from a SIMPLE 401(k) plan are permitted.

121. C

To be considered a "qualified purchaser," an individual must have not less than $5 million in investments.

122. C

A recourse loan is a type of debt that allows the lender to collect from the debtor and the debtor's assets in the case of default, as opposed to foreclosing on a particular property or asset.

123. A

There is an inverse relationship between the coupon rate of a bond and its duration. Therefore, the lower the coupon rate, the greater the bond's duration.

124. B
There is a direct relationship between the maturity date of a bond and its duration. Therefore, the longer the term to maturity, the greater the bond's duration.

125. A
There is an inverse relationship between the yield to maturity of a bond and its duration. Therefore, the lower the yield to maturity, the greater the bond's duration.

126. B
The NASAA (North American Securities Administrators Association) is the voice of state securities agencies responsible for efficient capital formation and grass-roots investor protection in the U.S. Their fundamental mission is to protect consumers who purchase securities or investment advice, and their jurisdiction extends to a wide variety of issuers and intermediaries who offer and sell securities to the public.

127. C
Unit investment trusts (UITs) are sold to investors for a typical cost of $1,000. Units may be bought or sold on the secondary market, and upon termination of a UIT, any remaining securities in the trust will be sold and proceeds will be paid to investors. They typically have low fees and expenses.

128 A
Contributions to a Roth IRA can be made at any age and are never deductible. A Roth IRA owner is not required to take a minimum distribution during his or her lifetime.

129. D
Firms must retain blotters containing all purchases and sales of securities for at least 6 years, and they must keep copies of confirmations for 3 years. For the first 2 years, these records must be kept in an easily accessible location.

130. A
TIPS (Treasury inflation-protected securities) are taxed at the federal level only.

PRACTICE EXAM 4

QUESTIONS

1. Which of the following are considered fiduciaries?

   (1) A retirement plan administrator, including any third-party administrator that is used by the employer.
   (2) A retirement plan sponsor/employer, including its officers and/or directors.
   (3) An investment adviser that renders advice to a retirement plan for a fee or other compensation.
   (4) A retirement plan trustee.

   A. (1) and (2) only
   B. (2) and (4) only
   C. (1), (2), and (3) only
   D. All of the above are correct.

2. Which of the following typically invest in high-quality, short-term investments, such as Treasury bills, commercial paper, and negotiable CDs? The underlying investments have an average maturity of 30 to 90 days.

   A. CDs
   B. Commercial paper
   C. Money market funds
   D. Treasury bonds

3. Which of the following is the formula to calculate an investment's real return?

   A. Real return = Nominal return – Inflation
   B. Real return = Nominal return + Inflation
   C. Real return = Nominal return ÷ Inflation
   D. Real return = Inflation ÷ Nominal return

4. All but which of the following are correct regarding the IARD?

   A. It was developed according to the requirements of its sponsors, the SEC and NASAA.
   B. Its database helps promote uniformity through the use of common forms, and efficiency through a paperless environment.
   C. It is to investment advisers what the CRD is to broker-dealers.
   D. All of the above are correct.

5. Which of the following describes the illegal practice of excessive buying and selling of securities in a customer's account without considering the customer's investment goals? Its primary goal is to generate commissions that benefit the broker.

   A. Capping
   B. Churning
   C. Front running
   D. Painting the tape

6. Which of the following is/are correct regarding liquidity and marketability?

    (1) Liquidity is the ability to sell or redeem an investment quickly and at a known price without incurring a significant loss of principal.
    (2) Marketability is the speed and ease with which an investment may be bought or sold.

    A. (1) only
    B. (2) only
    C. Both (1) and (2) are correct.
    D. Neither (1) or (2) are correct.

7. Which of the following are among the economic goals of the Federal Reserve and the U.S. Treasury?

    (1) Full employment
    (2) Stable prices
    (3) Economic growth
    (4) Decrease government spending

    A. (1) and (4) only
    B. (3) and (4) only
    C. (1), (2), and (3) only
    D. All of the above are correct.

8. Which of the following retirement plans would be most suitable to retain young employees?

    A. Cash balance plan
    B. Defined benefit plan
    C. Money purchase plan
    D. Target benefit plan

9. Which of the following is the largest options exchange in the U.S., and focuses on options contracts for individual equities and indexes?

    A. AMEX
    B. CBOE
    C. NASDAQ
    D. NYSE

10. Which of the following acts is designed to provide greater deterrence and punishment for people trading on material non-public information, and to improve detection of other perceived market abuses?

    A. Securities Act Amendments of 1975
    B. Insider Trading and Securities Fraud Enforcement Act of 1988
    C. National Securities Market Improvement Act of 1996
    D. Sarbanes-Oxley Act of 2002

11. The Dow Jones Industrial Average is an index comprised of _____ industrial com-
    Panies.

    A. 20
    B. 30
    C. 40
    D. 50

12. Which of the following is a type of mutual fund that invests only in the equity securi-
    ties of companies located outside the U.S.?

    A. Aggressive growth fund
    B. Balanced fund
    C. Global fund
    D. International fund

13. All but which of the following are characteristics of defined contribution plans?

    A. Employer contributions are defined.
    B. The employee assumes the risk of investment performance.
    C. The employer assumes the risk of pre-retirement inflation.
    D. Benefits cannot be provided for past service.

14. All but which of the following are among the three categories of firm communications
    that are defined and regulated by FINRA Rule 2210?

    A. Correspondence
    B. Institutional communication
    C. Marketing communication
    D. Retail communication

15. All but which of the following are considered qualitative data?

    A. Account balances
    B. Goals
    C. Lifestyle
    D. Needs

16. A _____ is issued by a governmental body to finance a specific project. It is not
    backed by the full faith and credit of the issuing body.

    A. general obligation bond
    B. multi-purpose bond
    C. private activity bond
    D. revenue bond

17. Which of the following is defined as the benefit provided to an asset manager by a broker-dealer as a result of commissions generated from financial transactions executed by the broker-dealer?

    A. 12b-1 compensation
    B. Administrative compensation
    C. Hard-dollar compensation
    D. Soft-dollar compensation

18. Which of the following is/are correct regarding registered bonds and bearer bonds?

    (1) A registered bond is registered with the corporation or organization that issued the bond, and coupon payments are made to the owner of record.
    (2) A bearer bond can be transferred like cash, and coupon payments are made to the person who holds the bond.

    A. (1) only
    B. (2) only
    C. Both (1) and (2) are correct.
    D. Neither (1) or (2) are correct.

19. Gifts made during a donor's lifetime receive a _____ of basis, and gifts made at death receive a _____ of basis.

    A. carryover, carryover
    B. carryover, step-up
    C. step-up, carryover
    D. step-up, step-up

20. Which of the following impose the reporting and disclosure requirements for defined benefit plans?

    A. ERISA
    B. IRS
    C. PBGC
    D. SEC

21. Which of the following is/are correct regarding interest paid from municipal bonds?

    (1) Interest paid from municipal bonds is not taxed by the federal government.
    (2) Interest paid from municipal bonds is never taxable at the state level.

    A. (1) only
    B. (2) only
    C. Both (1) and (2) are correct.
    D. Neither (1) or (2) are correct.

22. To promote and enhance cyber security, an RIA's Chief Compliance Officer should educate firm employees about which of the following fraudulent activities that involves obtaining financial or other confidential information from internet users, usually by sending an email that looks as though it has been sent by a legitimate organization? The email usually contains a link to a fake website that looks authentic.

   A. Phishing
   B. Spamming
   C. Spoofing
   D. Worming

23. Which of the following is an unconditional promise to pay a sum of money to a payee, either at a fixed or determinable future time, under specific terms?

   A. Bank draft
   B. IOU
   C. Promissory note
   D. None of the above are correct.

24. According to the "brochure rule," if there have been material changes in the brochure since the adviser's last annual updating amendment, the adviser must deliver either a current brochure or a summary of the material changes to each client within _____ of the end of the adviser's fiscal year.

   A. 30 days
   B. 60 days
   C. 90 days
   D. 120 days

25. A currency transaction report (CTR) is a report that U.S. financial institutions are required to file with which of the following?

   A. FinCEN
   B. FINRA
   C. NAIC
   D. NASD

26. Which of the following is/are correct regarding beta?

   (1) It is used to measure the amount of unsystematic risk in an investor's portfolio.
   (2) A portfolio's beta can be positive or equal to zero, but cannot be negative.

   A. (1) only
   B. (2) only
   C. Both (1) and (2) are correct.
   D. Neither (1) or (2) are correct.

27. Which of the following regulations contains rules providing exemptions from the registration requirements under the Securities Act of 1933?

    A. Regulation A
    B. Regulation G
    C. Regulation T
    D. Regulation U

28. Regarding the money supply, which of the following is the formula for M2?

    A. M2 = M1 + Savings accounts + Short-term time deposits
    B. M2 = M1 + Coins and currency in circulation + Money held in checking accounts
    C. M2 = M1 + Long-term time deposits
    D. M2 = M1 + Money held in checking accounts

29. An investment adviser that has custody of client assets must file an audited balance sheet with the SEC within how many days of the investment adviser's fiscal year end?

    A. 30 days
    B. 60 days
    C. 90 days
    D. 120 days

30. Which of the following acts is credited with forming the Municipal Securities Rulemaking Board (MSRB)?

    A. Securities Investor Protection Act of 1970
    B. Securities Act Amendments of 1975
    C. Uniform Prudent Investors Act of 1994
    D. National Securities Market Improvement Act of 1996

31. Which of the following describes a strategy used to minimize the interest rate risk of bond investments by adjusting the portfolio duration to match the investment time horizon?

    A. Bond hedging
    B. Bond immunization
    C. Bond laddering
    D. Bond spread

32. The Federal Reserve Board performs which of the following actions?

    A. It sets monetary policy, but does not set tax policy.
    B. It sets tax policy, but does not set monetary policy.
    C. It sets monetary policy and tax policy.
    D. None of the above are correct.

33. When a bond is selling at a premium to par, the yield to maturity (YTM) will always be _____ the bond's coupon rate. If a bond is selling at a discount to par, the YTM will always be _____ the bond's coupon rate.

    A. greater than, equal to
    B. greater than, less than
    C. less than, equal to
    D. less than, greater than

34. When an individual dies without a will and without family, the decedent's property will _____ to the state where he or she resided at the date of death.

    A. abate
    B. escheat
    C. estop
    D. reform

35. Which of the following bonds guarantees that the principal will act in accordance with certain laws, and if the principal fails to perform in this manner, the bond will cover resulting damages or losses?

    A. Bearer bond
    B. Brady bond
    C. Fidelity bond
    D. Surety bond

36. Emily creates an irrevocable trust to which she contributes income producing property. The trust will pay her income for life equal to 6% of the value of the trust revalued annually. At Emily's death, the trust corpus will be paid to a public charity. Which type of trust did Emma create?

    A. Charitable remainder annuity trust
    B. Charitable remainder unitrust
    C. Charitable lead unitrust
    D. Charitable lead annuity trust

37. In which of the following qualified retirement plans are the employees responsible for the investment risk?

    (1) Money purchase plans
    (2) Target benefit plans
    (3) Defined benefit plans
    (4) Cash balance plans

    A. (1) and (3) only
    B. (1) and (2) only
    C. (2) and (3) only
    D. (3) and (4) only

For questions 38 – 41, match the form of dividend with the description that follows. Use only one answer per blank. Answers may be used more than once or not at all.

    A. Stock dividend
    B. Credit dividend
    C. Ordinary dividend
    D. Qualified dividend
    E. Constructive dividend
    F. Liquidating dividend
    G. Tax dividend

38. ___ A distribution made by a corporation that is paid as additional shares of stock rather than cash.

39. ___ A type of dividend to which capital gains tax rates are applied.

40. ___ Normally a disguised dividend, such as a below-market shareholder loan.

41. ___ A payment to shareholders that exceeds the company's retained earnings; payment is made from capital rather than earnings.

42. An annual interest rate of 4.7% is equivalent to:

    A. 0.392% monthly or 1.175% quarterly.
    B. 0.392% monthly or 1.573% quarterly.
    C. 1.175% quarterly or 0.412% monthly.
    D. 2.352% quarterly or 0.783% monthly.

43. Which of the following is a characteristic of a debenture bond?

    A. Debenture bonds are secured bonds.
    B. Debenture bondholders have the same rights as general creditors.
    C. To account for the lower default risk, debenture bonds will have lower yields to maturity than secured bonds issued for the same term by the same issuer.
    D. All of the above are correct.

44. Earnings after taxes ÷ Total assets = _____

    A. Current ratio
    B. Net profit margin
    C. Return on assets
    D. Return on equity

45. If a portfolio has a beta of 1.0, what type of risk does the portfolio have?

    A. Diversifiable risk
    B. Non-systematic risk
    C. Systematic risk
    D. Both non-systematic and diversifiable risk

46. An investor who owns 5% cumulative preferred stock will receive a semiannual dividend of:

    A. $0.25 per share.
    B. $0.50 per share.
    C. $2.50 per share.
    D. $5.00 per share.

47. A skip person for generation-skipping transfer tax (GSTT) purposes is a related individual _____ below that of the transferor.

    A. one or more generations
    B. two or more generations
    C. 21 years
    D. 27.5 years

48. If an employer maintains a SIMPLE plan, which of the following plans can it also have in operation at the same time?

    A. 403(b) plan
    B. SEP
    C. Qualified plan
    D. None of the above are correct.

49. All but which of the following are correct regarding advertising activities engaged in by an RIA?

    A. Securities laws and rules prohibit performance advertising.
    B. Advertisements may not use or refer to testimonials.
    C. A testimonial refers to any statement of a client's experience or endorsement.
    D. All of the above are correct.

50. Which of the following mutual fund share classes will charge investors a back-end load?

    A. Class A shares
    B. Class B shares
    C. Class C shares
    D. Class D shares

51. Which of the following options will put an investor at the greatest risk?

    A. Buying a put while not owning the stock.
    B. Buying a put while owning the stock.
    C. Selling a stock short while not owning the stock.
    D. Selling a stock short while owning the stock.

52. If an investor expects a large decrease in the stock market 60 days from today, she can take advantage of the change by doing which of the following?

(1) Buying S&P 500 index calls
(2) Buying S&P 500 index puts
(3) Selling S&P 500 index calls
(4) Selling S&P 500 index puts

A. (1) and (3) only
B. (1) and (4) only
C. (2) and (3) only
D. (2) and (4) only

53. An investor purchased a 5-year bond that pays a 3.5% semiannual coupon payment. The bond is priced at $97 per $100 of par value. What is the bond's current yield?

A. 3.50%
B. 3.61%
C. 7.22%
D. 7.65%

The following information relates to questions 54 – 55.

Beta Corporation, a broker-dealer, would like to withdraw their state registration.

54. Which of the following forms must Beta Corporation submit to withdraw registration?

A. Form ADV-W
B. Form BDW
C. Form BR
D. Form W

55. The withdrawal will become effective _____ following the SEC's receipt of the form, unless the division notifies Beta Corporation otherwise.

A. 30 days
B. 60 days
C. 90 days
D. 120 days

56. Which of the following is correct regarding profit sharing plan allocation formulas?

A. Allocation formulas may discriminate in favor of highly compensated employees without penalty.
B. Contributions may not be skewed to favor older employees.
C. Allocation formulas must be definite and predetermined.
D. Employee contributions must be allocated on a pro-rata basis.

57. As a base country's currency strengthens relative to other countries, which of the following will result?

   A. The base country's exports will become less attractive to foreign consumers because the base country's goods are considered to be expensive.
   B. The base country's exports will become less attractive to foreign consumers because the base country's goods are considered to be cheap.
   C. The base country's exports will become more attractive to foreign consumers because the base country's goods are considered to be expensive.
   D. The base country's exports will remain unchanged because the strength or weakness of a country's currency does not affect exports.

58. In a joint tenancy between non-spouses, _____ of the property will be included in the gross estate of the decedent unless the survivor shows consideration furnished.

   A. 0%
   B. 25%
   C. 50%
   D. 100%

59. According to the Rule of 72, how many years will it take for an investment to double if the rate of return is 8% per year?

   A. 8 years
   B. 9 years
   C. 10 years
   D. 12 years

60. Rob owns 200 shares of Epsilon stock, which recently announced that it will pay a 4% stock dividend. How many shares will Rob have after the dividend has been paid?

   A. 192 shares
   B. 200 shares
   C. 204 shares
   D. 208 shares

61. Which of the following are permitted investments in a 403(b) plan?

   (1) Mutual funds
   (2) Bond funds
   (3) Treasury bills
   (4) Life insurance that is incidental to an annuity contract

   A. (1) and (4) only
   B. (2) and (3) only
   C. (1), (2), and (4) only
   D. All of the above are correct.

62. The initial margin percentage is currently _____ as established by Regulation T of the Federal Reserve Board.

   A. 25%
   B. 30%
   C. 50%
   D. 75%

63. All but which of the following are correct regarding counter-cyclical stocks?

   A. They perform better during economic downturns.
   B. They are negatively correlated to the overall state of the economy.
   C. Examples of counter-cyclical stocks include airlines and hotels.
   D. They outperform during the contraction phase of the business cycle.

64. Which of the following is the minimum age requirement to use the substantially equal period payment (SEPP) exception to the 10% premature distribution penalty from an IRA?

   A. Age 21
   B. Age 59 ½
   C. Age 65
   D. There is no minimum age requirement.

65. An investor purchases two puts. The first is a September Theta put at $35, underlying currently selling at $37. The second is a November Delta put at $28, underlying currently selling at $25. Ignoring transaction costs, what is the value of the options?

   A. Theta: –$2; Delta: $3
   B. Theta: $0; Delta: –$3
   C. Theta: $0; Delta: $3
   D. Theta: $2; Delta: $3

66. The duration of a bond is least affected by its:

   A. coupon.
   B. interest rate.
   C. quality.
   D. time to maturity.

67. Jessica would like to set up a revocable living trust but is concerned about potential adverse tax consequences. If she sets up a revocable living trust and places all of her income producing assets into the trust, how will the income from the trust be taxed?

   A. The income will pass through to the Jessica, who will pay it personally.
   B. The income will be taxed at trust tax rates.
   C. The income will accumulate tax-free within the trust.
   D. Part of the income will pass through to Jessica, who will pay it personally, and part of the income will accumulate tax-free within the trust.

68. An analyst provides the following information for an index comprised of 4 securities:

Security	Beginning of Period Price ($)	End of Period Price ($)
Security A	$38.00	$46.00
Security B	$29.00	$33.00
Security C	$50.00	$53.00
Security D	$80.00	$86.00

If the securities are part of a price-weighted index, what is the return of the index?

A. 10.66%
B. 12.09%
C. 13.63%
D. 14.29%

69. **Which of the following will result if money distributed from a 529 Plan is not used to pay for qualifying education expenses?**

A. The gain is taxed at capital gains rates, and a 10% penalty is applied.
B. The gain is taxed at capital gains rates, and a 20% penalty is applied.
C. The gain is taxed as ordinary income, and a 10% penalty is applied.
D. The gain is taxed as ordinary income, and a 20% penalty is applied.

70. **All but which of the following are correct regarding a convertible bond?**

A. It is a type of corporate bond that may be converted into common stock of the issuing corporation.
B. It may be converted at the bondholder's discretion.
C. It allows an investor to share in the growth of the corporation only if the bond is converted into common stock.
D. It is a zero-coupon bond issued at a discount to par.

71. **John owns an investment yielding an after-tax return of 9.5%. If he is in the 15% tax bracket, what is the equivalent pre-tax return?**

A. 1.43%
B. 8.08%
C. 10.93%
D. 11.18%

72. **Which of the following lines indicates the direction and speed that a security's price moves over a period of time?**

A. Capital market line
B. Security market line
C. Support line
D. Trendline

73. A doctor starting a new medical practice is concerned about limiting her personal liability. She would like to have flow-through taxation and the ability to easily sell interests in her practice in the future. Which of the following entities is most suitable for the doctor to meet her goals?

A. C Corp
B. S Corp
C. Sole proprietorship
D. Limited partnership

74. Which of the following is/are correct regarding support and resistance levels?

(1) Support is the level at which demand is strong enough to prevent security prices from rising further.
(2) Resistance is the level at which selling activity is strong enough to prevent security prices from declining further.

A. (1) only
B. (2) only
C. Both (1) and (2) are correct.
D. Neither (1) or (2) are correct.

75. If an investment is held for more than one year, the holding period return _____ the true investment return on an annual basis. If an investment is held for less than one year, the holding period return _____ the true investment return.

A. correctly states, overstates
B. overstates, correctly states
C. overstates, understates
D. understates, overstates

76. Which of the following is an advertisement used by a registered investment company that advises readers to obtain a full prospectus? It is not permitted to include an application to invest, and it must contain specific caveats pursuant to SEC Rule 482.

A. Omitting prospectus
B. Preliminary prospectus
C. Shelf registration
D. Tombstone ad

77. Long-term capital gains tax rates apply if an asset is held for:

A. at least 12 months.
B. longer than 12 months.
C. at least 6 months using the half-year convention.
D. longer than 6 months using the half-year convention.

78. Which of the following is an investment strategy entered into to reduce or offset the risk of adverse price movements in a security by taking an offsetting position in another investment?

   A. Arbitrage
   B. Derivative
   C. Hedge
   D. Option

79. Contractionary policy is characterized by which of the following?

   A. Increasing government borrowing
   B. Increasing public spending
   C. Increasing taxes
   D. All of the above are correct.

80. An individual who meets which of the following criteria must register as an investment adviser?

   (1) The individual provides advice or analyses concerning securities.
   (2) The individual is in the business of providing investment advice.
   (3) The individual provides investment advice for compensation.
   (4) The individual is a CPA or attorney whose investment advice is only incidental to his or her other activities.

   A. (3) only
   B. (1), (2), and (3) only
   C. (1), (2), and (4) only
   D. (2), (3), and (4) only

81. Which of the following can an investor sign which allows him or her to receive breakpoint discounts based upon a commitment to buy a specified number of mutual fund shares over a period of time, usually 13 months?

   A. Investment advisory contract
   B. Investment memorandum
   C. Letter of intent
   D. Prospectus

82. Bill, age 67, recently received a $650,000 inheritance from his uncle's estate. To provide sufficient income during retirement, he needs an annuity that will produce the highest payout for the rest of his life. Which settlement option should Bill select?

   A. Dollar certain
   B. Joint life
   C. Life with a 10-year period certain
   D. Single life

83. All but which of the following are characteristics of a C Corp?

    A. They are subject to double taxation.
    B. They have a perpetual life.
    C. They must have stock available for purchase on an exchange.
    D. They can potentially be classified as a personal service corporation (PSC).

84. Which of the following is correct regarding the interest paid by Treasury STRIPS?

    A. They pay interest monthly.
    B. They pay interest semiannually.
    C. They pay interest annually.
    D. They do not pay interest.

For questions 85 – 88, match the retirement plan with the description that follows. Use only one answer per blank. Each answer may be used only once.

    A. Profit sharing plan
    B. Money purchase plan
    C. Cash balance plan
    D. Target benefit plan

85. ___ A plan that requires a fixed percentage of compensation to be contributed for each eligible employee.

86. ___ A plan similar to a defined benefit plan because contributions are based on projected retirement benefits.

87. ___ A type of defined contribution plan that is not a pension plan.

88. ___ A defined benefit plan that defines an employee's benefit in terms that are more characteristic with a defined contribution plan.

89. Which of the following measures the level of trading activity within a mutual fund?

    A. Capitalization rate
    B. Expense rate
    C. Price/earnings rate
    D. Turnover rate

90. If an investment pays a monthly interest rate of 0.9%, it is equivalent to:

    A. 1.8% quarterly or 5.4% annually.
    B. 2.7% quarterly or 8.1% annually.
    C. 2.7% quarterly or 10.8% annually.
    D. 5.4% quarterly or 10.8% annually.

91. A hedge fund is a _____ offered fund of securities for high-net worth investors. The hedge fund manager is generally paid a _____ fee.

   A. privately, flat
   B. privately, performance
   C. publicly, flat
   D. publicly, performance

92. When a corporation files a registration with the SEC in an effort to sell shares to the public, the period of time between the filing of the registration statement and its effective date is referred to as the:

   A. cooling-off period.
   B. prospectus period.
   C. registration period.
   D. terminable interest period.

93. Last year, Alpha Holding Company reported an annual cost of goods sold of $17.6 million. Total assets increased by $12.1 million, including an increase of $1.1 million in inventory. Total liabilities increased by $9.9 million, including an increase of $440,000 in accounts payable. Based on this information, how much cash was paid to suppliers?

   A. $10.34 million
   B. $16.94 million
   C. $18.26 million
   D. $18.70 million

94. Which of the following is the measure of a company's earnings per share if all convertible securities were exercised and converted to common stock?

   A. Converted earnings per share
   B. Conversion ratio per share
   C. Diluted earnings per share
   D. Price/earnings per share

95. Which of the following describes actions taken by the Federal Reserve and their effect on the money supply?

   (1) If the Federal Reserve sells government securities, it receives money in return, which increases the money supply.
   (2) If the Federal Reserve sells government securities, it is considered contractionary policy.

   A. (1) only
   B. (2) only
   C. Both (1) and (2) are correct.
   D. Neither (1) or (2) are correct.

96. Which of the following is the electronic service that provides quotation information for stocks traded on the AMEX, NYSE, and other regional stock exchanges, and also includes issues traded by FINRA member firms in the third market?

A. Alternative Trading System
B. Consolidated Quotation System
C. National Service Clearing Corporation
D. Trade Reporting and Compliance Engine

97. For a defined contribution plan, annual contributions to an employee's account are limited to the lesser of _____ of compensation or _____ in 2018.

A. 20%, $18,500
B. 20%, $24,500
C. 25%, $55,000
D. 25%, $220,000

98. Which of the following is another name for conduit theory, which states that an investment company that passes all of its capital gains, interest, and dividends through to shareholders shouldn't be taxed at the corporate level?

A. Corporate tax theory
B. Passive income theory
C. Passthrough theory
D. Pipeline theory

99. When an economy is experiencing inflation, an overall _____ in consumer prices leads to a _____ of purchasing power.

A. decrease, decrease
B. decrease, increase
C. increase, decrease
D. increase, increase

100. The gift tax annual exclusion is permitted for:

(1) present interest gifts only.
(2) future interest gifts only.
(3) present and future interest gifts.
(4) any completed gift that does not revert back to the grantor.

A. (1) only
B. (3) only
C. (3) and (4) only
D. (1), (3), and (4) only

101. Which of the following acts regulates the organization of companies, including mutual funds, that engage primarily in investing, reinvesting, and trading in securities? The act is designed to minimize conflicts of interest that arise in these complex operations.

    A. Securities Exchange Act of 1934
    B. Trust Indenture Act of 1939
    C. Investment Company Act of 1940
    D. Uniform Securities Act of 1956

102. Which of the following is a system that automates and standardizes procedures for the transfer of assets in a customer account from one brokerage firm and/or bank to another?

    A. ACATS
    B. ECN
    C. TRACE
    D. WIRE

103. The Trust Indenture Act of 1939 prohibits bond issues over _____ from being offered for sale without a formal agreement signed by both the bond issuer and the bondholder that fully discloses the details of the issue.

    A. $1 million
    B. $5 million
    C. $10 million
    D. $15 million

104. Which of the following is/are correct regarding investment risk in a qualified retirement plan?

    (1) In a defined contribution plan, the employer bears the investment risk.
    (2) In a defined benefit plan, the employee bears the investment risk.

    A. (1) only
    B. (2) only
    C. Both (1) and (2) are correct.
    D. Neither (1) or (2) are correct.

105. Which of the following are among the criteria to be an "accredited investor"?

    A. Net worth exceeding $500,000, either alone or together with a spouse, excluding the value of the person's primary residence.
    B. Net worth exceeding $500,000, either alone or together with a spouse, including the value of the person's primary residence.
    C. Net worth exceeding $1,000,000, either alone or together with a spouse, excluding the value of the person's primary residence.
    D. Net worth exceeding $1,000,000, either alone or together with a spouse, including the value of the person's primary residence.

106. Which of the following are among the exemptions from the 10% early withdrawal penalty from an IRA?

(1) Higher education costs for the account owner's child.
(2) Hardship withdrawals.
(3) A first-time home purchase up to $10,000.
(4) Separation from employment service at age 55 or older.
(5) A loan for medical expenses.

A. (1) and (3) only
B. (2) and (4) only
C. (3) and (5) only
D. (1), (3), and (4) only

For questions 107 – 109, match the real estate investment with the description that follows. Use only one answer per blank. Answers may be used more than once or not at all.

A. Equity REIT
B. Mortgage REIT
C. REMIC

107. ___ Invests in loans secured by real estate.

108. ___ Self-liquidating, flow-through entity that invests in real estate mortgages or mortgage-backed securities.

109. ___ Acquires ownership interests in commercial, industrial, and residential properties. Income is received from the rental of these properties.

110. Which of the following yield curves results from short-term debt instruments having a higher yield than long-term debt instruments of the same credit quality?

A. Flat yield curve
B. Inverted yield curve
C. Normal yield curve
D. Steep yield curve

111. The Federal Trade Commission implemented which of the following rules that requires broker-dealers and other financial institutions to create a written identity theft prevention program designed to detect the warning signs of identity theft in their day-to-day operations?

A. CTR Rule
B. Red Flags Rule
C. SRO Rule
D. Whistleblower Rule

112. Inflation is measured by which of the following?

   A. CPI
   B. GNI
   C. GNP
   D. NNI

113. Which of the following is a requirement in which financial institutions need to verify the identity of individuals wishing to conduct financial transactions with them?

   A. Automated Client Account Transfer Service
   B. Customer Identification Program
   C. Trade Reporting and Compliance Engine
   D. None of the above are correct.

114. Which of the following is a model statute designed to guide each state in drafting its state securities laws? It was created by the National Conference of Commissioners on Uniform State Laws.

   A. Maloney Act
   B. Patriot Act
   C. Uniform Prudent Investors Act
   D. Uniform Securities Act

The following information relates to questions 115 – 117.

Kappa Fund has recorded the following investment returns for the past seven years: –3%, +4%, +5%, –3%, +2%, +6%, –1%

115. Which of the following is the mean return?

   A. 1.43%
   B. 1.67%
   C. 1.81%
   D. 1.98%

116. Which of the following is the median?

   A. –3%
   B. –1%
   C. 2%
   D. 6%

117. Which of the following is the mode?

   A. –3%
   B. –1%
   C. 2%
   D. 6%

118. Book value is calculated through which of the following formulas?

    A. Book value = Total assets – (Intangible assets + Liabilities)
    B. Book value = Tangible assets + Intangible assets – Liabilities
    C. Book value = Total assets – (Intangible assets – Liabilities)
    D. Book value = Tangible assets – Intangible assets + Liabilities

119. The difference between a bond's price and the conversion parity price is referred to as which of the following?

    A. Bond premium
    B. Conversion premium
    C. Discount price
    D. Option premium

120. Which of the following SEC regulations require member firms that offer or maintain covered accounts to develop and implement written identity theft prevention programs?

    A. Regulation BB
    B. Regulation CF
    C. Regulation FD
    D. Regulation S-ID

121. Which of the following is correct regarding Electronic Communication Networks (ECNs)?

    A. All registered investment advisers are permitted to become ECN subscribers.
    B. ECNs are not permitted to become members of FINRA.
    C. An execution occurs when the price of a buy order and the price of a sell order intersect on the ECN.
    D. All of the above are correct.

122. The two main types of mutual fund prospectuses are the _____ prospectus and the _____ prospectus.

    A. omitting, statutory
    B. preliminary, statutory
    C. preliminary, summary
    D. statutory, summary

123. Which of the following is the world's largest equity derivatives clearing organization? By acting as guarantor, they ensure that the obligations of the contracts that they clear are fulfilled.

    A. AMBAC
    B. NASDAQ
    C. NSCC
    D. OCC

124. Which of the following is a person who, for compensation, makes recommendations regarding securities, manages client accounts, and determines which advice regarding securities should be given?

A. ADV
B. CRD
C. IAR
D. IARD

For questions 125 – 128, match the type of stock with the description that follows. Use only one answer per blank. Answers may be used more than once or not at all.

A. Cyclical stocks
B. Defensive stocks

125. ___ Pharmaceutical companies

126. ___ Automobiles

127. ___ Airlines

128. ___ Railroads

129. Which of the following are activity ratios?

(1) Inventory turnover ratio
(2) Average collection period
(3) Fixed asset turnover ratio
(4) Debt-to-equity ratio

A. (1) and (4) only
B. (1), (2), and (3) only
C. (2), (3), and (4) only
D. All of the above are correct.

130. Which of the following is/are correct regarding profit sharing plans?

(1) Profit sharing plans are a type of defined contribution pension plan.
(2) The minimum funding standard requires the employer to make an annual contribution.

A. (1) only
B. (2) only
C. Both (1) and (2) are correct.
D. Neither (1) or (2) are correct.

ANSWER KEY

1. D
A fiduciary includes a retirement plan administrator, including any third-party administrator that is used by the employer; a retirement plan sponsor/employer, including its officers and/or directors; an investment adviser that renders advice to a retirement plan for a fee or other compensation; and a retirement plan trustee.

2. C
Money market funds typically invest in high-quality, short-term investments, such as Treasury bills, commercial paper, and negotiable CDs. The underlying investments have an average maturity of 30 to 90 days.

3. A
Real return = Nominal return − Inflation

4. D
The IARD was developed according to the requirements of its sponsors, the SEC and NASAA. Its database helps promote uniformity through the use of common forms, and efficiency through a paperless environment. It is to investment advisers what the CRD is to broker-dealers.

5. B
Churning describes the illegal practice of excessive buying and selling of securities in a customer's account without considering the customer's investment goals. Its primary goal is to generate commissions that benefit the broker.

6. C
Liquidity is the ability to sell or redeem an investment quickly and at a known price without incurring a significant loss of principal. Marketability is the speed and ease with which an investment may be bought or sold.

7. C
The goals of the Federal Reserve and the U.S. Treasury are full employment, stable prices, and economic growth.

8. C
The cash balance plan, defined benefit plan, and target benefit plan all favor older employees. The money purchase plan favors younger employees.

9. B
The CBOE (Chicago Board Options Exchange) is the largest options exchange in the U.S. and focuses on options contracts for individual equities and indexes.

10. B
The Insider Trading and Securities Fraud Enforcement Act of 1988 is designed to provide greater deterrence and punishment for people trading on material non-public information, and to improve detection of other perceived market abuses.

11. B
The Dow Jones Industrial Average is an index comprised of 30 industrial companies.

12. D
International mutual funds invest in the equity securities of companies located outside the U.S. Global mutual funds invest in both international and domestic companies.

13. C
In a defined contribution plan, employer contributions are defined, and benefits cannot be provided for past service. The employee assumes the risk of investment performance and pre-retirement inflation.

14. C
The three categories of firm communications that are defined and regulated by FINRA Rule 2210 are correspondence, institutional communication, and retail communication.

15. A
Goals, lifestyle, and needs are considered qualitative data. Account balances are quantitative data.

16. D
A revenue bond is issued by a governmental body to finance a specific project. It is not backed by the full faith and credit of the issuing body. Instead, debts are repaid from revenue generated from the project that was financed.

17. D
Soft-dollar compensation is defined as the benefit provided to an asset manager by a broker-dealer as a result of commissions generated from financial transactions executed by the broker-dealer.

18. C
A registered bond is registered with the corporation or organization that issued the bond, and coupon payments are made to the owner of record. A bearer bond can be transferred like cash, and coupon payments are made to the person who holds the bond.

19. B
Gifts made during a donor's lifetime receive a carryover of basis, and gifts made at death receive a step-up of basis.

20. A
ERISA imposes the reporting and disclosure requirements for defined benefit plans.

21. A
Interest paid from municipal bonds is not taxed by the federal government. The bond interest may also be tax-exempt by various states if certain requirements are met.

22. A
Phishing is a fraudulent activity that involves obtaining financial or other confidential information from internet users, usually by sending an email that looks as though it has been sent by a legitimate organization. The email usually contains a link to a fake website that looks authentic.

23. C
A promissory note is an unconditional promise to pay a sum of money to a payee, either at a fixed or determinable future time, under specific terms. An IOU differs from a promissory note in that an IOU does not specify repayment terms such as the time of repayment. A bank draft is a type of check in which the payment is guaranteed to be available by the issuing bank.

24. D
According to the "brochure rule," if there have been material changes in the brochure since the adviser's last annual updating amendment, the adviser must deliver either a current brochure or a summary of the material changes to each client within 120 days of the end of the adviser's fiscal year.

25. A
A currency transaction report (CTR) is a report that U.S. financial institutions are required to file with FinCEN (Financial Crimes Enforcement Network).

26. D
Beta is used to measure the amount of systematic risk in an investor's portfolio. A portfolio's beta can be positive, negative, or equal to zero.

27. A
Regulation A contains rules providing exemptions from the registration requirements under the Securities Act of 1933.

28. A
M2 = M1 + Savings accounts + Short-term time deposits

29. C
An investment adviser that has custody of client assets must file an audited balance sheet with the SEC within 90 days of the investment adviser's fiscal year end.

30. B
The Securities Act Amendments of 1975 created the Municipal Securities Rulemaking Board (MSRB).

31. B
Bond immunization is an investment strategy used to minimize the interest rate risk of bond investments by adjusting the portfolio duration to match the investment time horizon.

32. A
The Federal Reserve Board sets monetary policy, but does not set tax policy.

33. D
When a bond is selling at a premium to par, the yield to maturity (YTM) will always be less than the bond's coupon rate. If a bond is selling at a discount to par, the YTM will always be greater than the bond's coupon rate.

34. B
When an individual dies without a will and without family, the decedent's property will escheat (pass) to the state where he or she resided at the date of death.

35. D
A surety bond guarantees that the principal will act in accordance with certain laws, and if the principal fails to perform in this manner, the bond will cover resulting damages or losses.

36. B
The trust described is a charitable remainder unitrust (CRUT) because the value of the trust is revalued annually.

37. B
The employee assumes the investment risk in a defined contribution plan. Money purchase plans and target benefit plans are types of defined contribution plans.

38. A
Stock dividends are distributions by a corporation that are paid as additional shares of stock rather than cash.

39. D
A qualified dividend is a type of dividend to which capital gains tax rates are applied.

40. E
A disguised dividend, such as a below-market shareholder loan, is considered to be a constructive dividend.

41. F
A payment to shareholders that exceeds the company's retained earnings is a liquidating dividend. The payment is made from capital rather than earnings.

42. A
Monthly interest rate = 4.7% ÷ 12 months = 0.392%
Quarterly interest rate = 4.7% ÷ 4 quarters = 1.175%

43. B
Debenture bonds are unsecured bonds, and debenture bondholders have the same rights as general creditors. To account for the higher default risk, debenture bonds will have higher yields to maturities than secured bonds issued for the same term by the same issuer.

44. C
Earnings after taxes ÷ Total assets = Return on assets

45. C
A portfolio with a beta of 1.0 will move in the same direction as the overall stock market. Therefore, the portfolio has only market risk, also known as systematic risk.

46. C
An investor who owns 5% cumulative preferred stock will receive a semiannual dividend of $2.50 per share.

47. B
A skip person for GSTT purposes is a related individual two or more generations below that of the transferor.

48. D
An employer cannot maintain any other qualified plan, 403(b) plan, or SEP at the same time that it has a SIMPLE plan in operation.

49. A
Advertisements by an RIA may not use or refer to testimonials, which refers to any statement of a client's experience or endorsement. Securities laws and rules do not prohibit performance advertising.

50. B
Class B mutual fund shares charge a back-end load.

51. C
Selling a stock short without already owning the stock would put an investor at the greatest risk. If the stock increases in value, the investor would have to repurchase the stock on the open market. However, if the investor already owned the stock, she would benefit from the shares appreciating in value.

52. C
If an investor expects a large decrease in the stock market 60 days from today, she can take advantage of the change by buying S&P 500 index puts and selling S&P 500 index calls.

53. B
Current yield = Sum of coupon payments ÷ Market price
Current yield = ($100 × 0.035) ÷ $97 = 0.0361 = 3.61%

54. B
Beta Corporation must submit Form BDW to withdraw their state registration.

55. A
The withdrawal will become effective 30 days following the SEC's receipt of the form, unless the division notifies Beta Corporation otherwise.

56. C
For a profit sharing plan, contributions may be skewed to favor older participants through methods such as age-weighting and cross-testing. Therefore, contributions do not need to be allocated on a pro-rata basis. The allocation formula cannot be discriminatory. Although profit sharing contributions must be substantial and recurring, the allocation formula must still be definite and predetermined.

57. A
As a base country's currency strengthens relative to other countries, the base country's exports will become less attractive to foreign consumers because the base country's goods are considered to be expensive.

58. D
In a joint tenancy between non-spouses, 100% of the property will be included in the gross estate of the decedent unless the survivor shows consideration furnished.

59. B
$72 \div 8 = 9$ years
By dividing 72 by the annual rate of return, an investor can determine how many years it will take for the initial investment to double.

60. D
200 shares + (200 shares × 0.04) = 208 shares

61. C
Mutual funds, bonds funds, and life insurance that is incidental to an annuity contract are permitted investments in a 403(b) plan.

62. C
The initial margin percentage is currently 50% as established by Regulation T of the Federal Reserve Board.

63. C
Counter-cyclical stocks perform better during economic downturns because they are negatively correlated to the overall state of the economy. They outperform during the contraction phase of the business cycle. Examples of counter-cyclical stocks include debt collectors, discount retailers, and alcoholic beverage manufacturers.

64. D
The substantially equal periodic payment (SEPP) exception to the 10% premature distribution penalty has no minimum age requirement.

65. C
The Theta option is out-of-the-money, therefore its value is $0. The value of the Delta option is $28 – $25 = $3.

66. C
The duration of a bond is least effected by its quality. There is an inverse relationship between interest rates, coupon payments, and duration. As interest rates and coupon payments decrease, duration increases. There is a direct relationship between time to maturity and duration. The longer the time to maturity, the longer the duration.

67. A
In a revocable living trust, income is passed through to the individual who will pay it personally. The trust itself is tax-neutral.

68. A
The price return of a price-weighted index is the percentage change in price of the index.
Step 1: $38 + $29 + $50 + $80 = $197
Step 2: $46 + $33 + $53 + $86 = $218
Step 3: ($218 – $197) ÷ $197 = 0.1066 = 10.66%

69. C
If money distributed from a 529 plan is not used to pay for qualifying education expenses, the gain is taxed as ordinary income and a 10% penalty is applied.

70. D
A convertible bond is a type of corporate bond that may be converted into common stock of the issuing corporation at the bondholder's discretion. It allows an investor to share in the growth of the corporation only if the bond is converted into common stock.

71. D
Pre-tax return = 0.095 ÷ (1 – 0.15) = 0.1118 = 11.18%

72. D
The trendline indicates the direction and speed that a security's price moves over a period of time.

73. B
A C Corp would not provide flow-through taxation as the doctor requested. A sole proprietorship would not limit her liability. A limited partnership may be appropriate, but there is no mention of a general partner. The best answer is the S Corp.

74. D
Support is the level at which demand is strong enough to prevent security prices from declining further. Resistance is the level at which selling activity is strong enough to prevent security prices from rising further.

75. C
If an investment is held for more than one year, the holding period return overstates the true investment return on an annual basis. If an investment is held for less than one year, the holding period return understates the true investment return.

76. A
An omitting prospectus is an advertisement used by a registered investment company that advises readers to obtain a full prospectus. It is not permitted to include an application to invest, and it must contain specific caveats pursuant to SEC Rule 482.

77. B
Long-term capital gains tax rates apply if an asset is held for longer than 12 months (at least 12 months and a day).

78. B
A derivative is an investment strategy entered into to reduce or offset the risk of adverse price movements in a security by taking an offsetting position in another investment.

79. C
Contractionary policy is characterized by increasing taxes, decreasing government borrowing, and decreasing public spending.

80. B
An individual who meets the following criteria must register as an investment adviser:
(1) The individual provides advice or analyses concerning securities.
(2) The individual is in the business of providing investment advice.
(3) The individual provides investment advice for compensation.

81. C
An investor can sign a letter of intent (LOI) which allows him or her to receive breakpoint discounts based upon a commitment to buy a specified number of mutual fund shares over a period of time, usually 13 months.

82. D
A single life annuity will provide the maximum payout to Bill. A single life annuity is also referred to as a "pure life" annuity.

83. C
A C Corp is subject to double taxation, has a perpetual life, and could potentially be classified as a personal service corporation (PSC).

84. D
Treasury STRIPS do not pay interest prior to maturity.

85. B
A money purchase plan requires a fixed percentage of compensation to be contributed for each eligible employee.

86. D
A target benefit plan is similar to a defined benefit plan because contributions are based on projected retirement benefits.

87. A
A profit sharing plan is a type of defined contribution plan that is not a pension plan.

88. C
A cash balance plan is a defined benefit plan that defines an employee's benefit in terms that are more characteristic with a defined contribution plan.

89. D
The turnover rate measures the level of trading activity within a mutual fund.

90. C
Quarterly interest rate = 0.9% × 3 months = 2.7%
Annual interest rate = 0.9% × 12 months = 10.8%

91. B

A hedge fund is a privately offered fund of securities for high-net worth investors. The hedge fund manager is generally paid a performance fee.

92. A

When a corporation files a registration with the SEC in an effort to sell shares to the public, the period of time between the filing of the registration statement and its effective date is referred to as the cooling-off period.

93. C

Cash paid to suppliers = Cost of goods sold + Increase in inventory – Increase in accounts payable

Cash paid to suppliers = $17.6 million + $1.1 million – $440,000 = $18.26 million

94. C

Diluted earnings per share is the measure of a company's earnings per share if all convertible securities were exercised and converted to common stock.

95. B

If the Federal Reserve sells government securities, it receives money in return, which reduces the money supply. This is considered contractionary policy.

96. B

The Consolidated Quotation System (CQS) is the electronic service that provides quotation information for stocks traded on the AMEX, NYSE, and other regional stock exchanges, and also includes issues traded by FINRA member firms in the third market.

97. C

For a defined contribution plan, annual contributions to an employee's account are limited to the lesser of 25% of compensation or $55,000 in 2018.

98. D

Pipeline theory is another name for conduit theory, which states that an investment company that passes all of its capital gains, interest, and dividends through to shareholders shouldn't be taxed at the corporate level.

99. C

When an economy is experiencing inflation, an overall increase in consumer prices leads to a decrease of purchasing power.

100. A

The gift tax annual exclusion is permitted for present interest gifts only.

101. C

The Investment Company Act of 1940 regulates the organization of companies, including mutual funds, that engage primarily in investing, reinvesting, and trading in securities. The act is designed to minimize conflicts of interest that arise in these complex operations.

102. A
The Automated Client Account Transfer Service (ACATS) is a system that automates and standardizes procedures for the transfer of assets in a customer account from one brokerage firm and/or bank to another.

103. B
The Trust Indenture Act of 1939 prohibits bond issues over $5 million from being offered for sale without a formal agreement signed by both the bond issuer and the bondholder that fully discloses the details of the issue.

104. D
In a defined contribution plan, the employee bears the investment risk. In a defined benefit plan, the employer bears the investment risk.

105. C
To be considered an accredited investor, net worth must exceed $1,000,000, either alone or together with a spouse, excluding the value of the person's primary residence.

106. A
Qualified education costs and a first-time home purchase are among the exemptions from the 10% early withdrawal penalty from an IRA. Hardship withdrawals, and withdrawals made after separating from employment service at age 55 or older are permitted in 401(k) plans but not IRAs. Loans from IRAs are not allowed.

107. B
Mortgage REITs invest in loans secured by real estate.

108. C
A REMIC is a self-liquidating, flow-through entity that invests in real estate mortgages or mortgage-backed securities.

109. A
Equity REITs acquire ownership interests in commercial, industrial, and residential properties. Income is received from the rental of these properties.

110. B
An inverted yield curve results from short-term debt instruments having a higher yield than long-term debt instruments of the same credit quality.

111. B
The Federal Trade Commission implemented the Red Flags Rule that requires broker-dealers and other financial institutions to create a written identity theft prevention program designed to detect the warning signs of identity theft in their day-to-day operations.

112. A
Inflation is measured by the CPI (Consumer Price Index).

113. B

The Customer Identification Program (CIP) is a requirement in which financial institutions need to verify the identity of individuals wishing to conduct financial transactions with them.

114. D

The Uniform Securities Act was created by the National Conference of Commissioners on Uniform State Laws, and is a model statute designed to guide each state in drafting its state securities laws.

115. A

Mean $= [(-3\%) + (4\%) + (5\%) + (-3\%) + (2\%) + (6\%) + (-1\%)] \div 7 = 1.43\%$

116. C

Median $= -3\%, -3\%, -1\%, +2\%, +4\%, +5\%, +6\% = 2\%$

117. A

−3% is the only number that appears twice, therefore it is the mode.

118. A

Book value = Total assets − (Intangible assets + Liabilities)

119. B

The difference between a bond's price and the conversion parity price is referred to as the conversion premium.

120. D

Regulation S-ID requires member firms that offer or maintain covered accounts to develop and implement written identity theft prevention programs.

121. C

ECNs are members of FINRA, and, typically, only broker-dealers and certain institutional traders are permitted to become ECN subscribers. An execution occurs when the price of a buy order and the price of a sell order intersect on the ECN.

122. D

The two main types of mutual fund prospectuses are the statutory prospectus and the summary prospectus.

123. D

The OCC (Options Clearing Corporation) is the world's largest equity derivatives clearing organization. By acting as guarantor, they ensure that the obligations of the contracts that they clear are fulfilled.

124. C

An IAR (investment adviser representative) is a person who, for compensation, makes recommendations regarding securities, manages client accounts, and determines which advice regarding securities should be given.

125. B
Pharmaceutical companies are defensive stocks.

126. A
Automobiles are cyclical stocks.

127. A
Airlines are cyclical stocks.

128. A
Railroads are cyclical stocks.

129. B
The activity ratios are the inventory turnover ratio, average collection period, and fixed asset turnover ratio.

130. D
A profit sharing plan is a type of defined contribution plan other than a pension plan. Contributions must be substantial and recurring, but are not required annually.

PRACTICE EXAM 5

QUESTIONS

1. Which of the following is an offering of shares to existing stockholders on a pro-rata basis?

   A. Private placement
   B. Public offering
   C. Rights offering
   D. Tender offering

2. Which of the following is correct regarding open market operations?

   A. It is a tool used by the Federal Reserve to implement monetary policy.
   B. It is conducted by the Trading Desk at the Federal Reserve Bank of New York.
   C. The authority to conduct open market operations is found in Section 14 of the Federal Reserve Act.
   D. All of the above are correct.

3. All but which of the following are characteristics of REMICs?

   A. They have a perpetual life.
   B. They combine the predictable cash flow of a bond with the high yield of a mortgage-backed security.
   C. Investors receive a specified cash flow from the underlying mortgages.
   D. They are self-liquidating.

4. Which of the following is an order to sell a stock at a price below the current market price?

   A. Sell discount order
   B. Sell limit order
   C. Sell market order
   D. Sell stop order

5. As a cyber security measure, broker-dealers should utilize a/an _____, which means that each time a user attempts to log into an investment account through an unrecognized device, the investment firm will send a unique code to the user via email or text message. Before the user can access the account, he or she must enter the code and password.

   A. access control
   B. declaration of conformity
   C. inspection certification
   D. two-step verification process

6. Justin, age 58, contributes to his employer's 401(k). In 2018, he will contribute $24,500 to the plan through salary deferrals, and he would like to contribute to an IRA as well. If he is single and has an income of $250,000, the maximum IRA contribution that he can make is:

A. $5,500 to a deductible IRA.
B. $6,500 to a deductible IRA.
C. $6,500 to a non-deductible IRA.
D. $6,500 to a Roth IRA.

7. When an investment company puts home mortgages or other loans into a pool and then sells securities representing shares of the pool, the securities sold are referred to as which of the following?

A. Asset-backed securities
B. Dark pools
C. Derivative-backed securities
D. Unit investment trusts

8. If the yield curve is _____, then the spread between yields of short-term and long-term bonds is _____.

A. flattening, decreasing
B. flattening, increasing
C. steepening, decreasing
D. steepening, increasing

9. Which of the following is also referred to as a "red herring?"

A. Omitting prospectus
B. Preliminary prospectus
C. Shelf registration
D. Tombstone ad

10. Which of the following investment strategies will expose an investor to the greatest amount of risk?

A. Buying a covered call
B. Buying a naked call
C. Selling a covered call
D. Selling a naked call

11. A quarterly interest rate of 3.2% is equivalent to:

A. 1.07% monthly or 9.60% annually.
B. 1.07% monthly or 12.80% annually.
C. 6.40% monthly or 9.60% annually.
D. 6.40% monthly or 12.80% annually.

12. All but which of the following are correct regarding the Federal Reserve?

    A. It derives its authority from Congress.
    B. It operates and oversees the U.S. payment system.
    C. It operates and oversees government spending.
    D. It supervises and regulates banks.

13. All but which of the following is another name for an income statement?

    A. Statement of financial performance
    B. Statement of financial position
    C. Statement of operations
    D. Statement of profit or loss

14. Which of the following is correct regarding the relationship between an investment's real return and nominal return?

    (1) Real return is an investment's rate of return after adjusting for inflation.
    (2) Nominal return is an investment's rate of return without adjusting for inflation.

    A. (1) only
    B. (2) only
    C. Both (1) and (2) are correct.
    D. Neither (1) or (2) are correct.

15. Which of the following theories states that security prices in different markets will not differ for any significant period of time?

    A. Arbitrage pricing theory
    B. Black-scholes valuation theory
    C. Efficient market theory
    D. Modern portfolio theory

16. Which of the following are required to obtain a viatical settlement?

    (1) The insured must not be terminally ill.
    (2) The insured must have owned the policy for at least one year.
    (3) The current beneficiary of the policy must sign a release or waiver.
    (4) The insured must sign a release allowing the viatical settlement provider access to his or her medical records.

    A. (1) and (2) only
    B. (3) and (4) only
    C. (2), (3), and (4) only
    D. All of the above are correct.

17. Which of the following is true regarding a qualified domestic trust (QDOT)?

    A. There must be at least one trustee who is a U.S. citizen or a qualifying domestic corporation.
    B. The surviving spouse must have the right to all income, as well as a general power of appointment over trust assets.
    C. The trust does not qualify for the marital deduction unless a special election is made by the trustee.
    D. Property in the trust is not subject to gift or estate taxes.

18. Which of the following are primary issuers of individual bonds?

    (1) Local government
    (2) U.S. government
    (3) An agency of the U.S. government
    (4) Corporations

    A. (1) and (4) only
    B. (1), (2), and (3) only
    C. (2), (3), and (4) only
    D. All of the above are correct.

The following information relates to questions 19 – 21.

Jennifer's income is $80,000 and she is in the 25% tax bracket. While preparing to file her tax return, she expected to take an $8,000 deduction through a government incentive program that she qualified for. However, she has discovered the deduction has been replaced with a $4,000 tax credit.

19. Ignoring exemptions and other adjustments, if Jennifer had claimed the $8,000 tax deduction, her total taxes owed would have been:

    A. $14,000.
    B. $16,000.
    C. $18,000.
    D. $20,000.

20. Ignoring exemptions and other adjustments, if Jennifer claims the $4,000 tax credit, her total taxes owed will be:

    A. $14,000.
    B. $16,000.
    C. $18,000.
    D. $20,000.

21. Ignoring exemptions and other adjustments, a tax credit of _____ would result in the same amount of taxes owed as the $8,000 tax deduction.

    A. $2,000
    B. $3,000
    C. $5,000
    D. $6,000

22. Which of the following is the formula to calculate a mutual fund's turnover rate?

    A. Turnover rate = Gross proceeds from sale of securities ÷ NAV
    B. Turnover rate = Gross proceeds from sale of securities – NAV
    C. Turnover rate = Gross proceeds from sale of securities + NAV
    D. Turnover rate = NAV ÷ Gross proceeds from sale of securities

23. Higher inflation = _____ interest rates = _____ bond values

    A. higher, higher
    B. higher, lower
    C. lower, higher
    D. lower, lower

24. If a wash sale occurs, which of the following will result?

    A. No loss deduction is allowed, and the amount of the disallowed loss is subtracted from the cost basis of the newly acquired shares.
    B. No loss deduction is allowed, and a gain must be realized immediately.
    C. No loss deduction is allowed, and the amount of the disallowed loss is added to the cost basis of the newly acquired shares.
    D. The loss can be realized.

25. Lisa, a single taxpayer with an AGI of $140,000, is permitted to fully deduct her IRA contribution if she's an active participant in which of the following plans?

    A. 401(k) plan with no match
    B. 403(b) plan with no match
    C. 403(b) plan with match
    D. 457 plan

26. If real GDP declined the last 3 quarters, how many more consecutive quarters of decline would be needed to be classified as an economic depression?

    A. 1 quarter
    B. 2 quarters
    C. 3 quarters
    D. 4 quarters

27. Which of the following is the ethical barrier that is required between different divisions of a financial institution to avoid conflicts of interest?

    A. Checks and balance system
    B. Chinese wall
    C. Ethical wall
    D. Moral barrier

28. Preferred stock that does not have to pay missed dividends is considered which of the following?

    A. Convertible
    B. Cumulative
    C. In-kind
    D. Noncumulative

29. Which of the following rules addresses the registration and resale requirements for securities issued in a merger, consolidation, acquisition of assets, or reclassification of securities?

    A. Securities Act Rule 145
    B. Securities Act Rule 172
    C. Securities Act Rule 238
    D. Securities Act Rule 405

30. The "cooling-off period," which transpires between the filing of a new issue's prospectus and the actual offering of the issue, must be a minimum of how many days?

    A. 7 days
    B. 10 days
    C. 20 days
    D. 30 days

31. Brady bonds are typically issued by which of the following countries?

    A. Asian countries
    B. European countries
    C. Latin American countries
    D. Middle Eastern countries

32. Expansionary policy is characterized by which of the following?

    A. Decreasing transfer payments
    B. Increasing public spending
    C. Increasing taxes
    D. All of the above are correct.

33. In order to maintain a SIMPLE plan, an employer may not have more than _____ employees.

    A. 25
    B. 50
    C. 75
    D. 100

34. An investment-grade bond is one that is rated _____ or higher by the Standard & Poor's bond rating service. A high-yield bond is rated _____ or lower by Standard & Poor's.

    A. BBB, BB
    B. BBB+, BB-
    C. BBB-, BB+
    D. BB, BBB

35. Which of the following has the most stable cash flows and the lowest prepayment risk of any class of CMO?

    A. General obligation bond
    B. Planned amortization class bond
    C. Targeted amortization class bond
    D. Zero-coupon bond

36. Blue sky laws are classified as which of the following?

    A. Federal-based laws
    B. International-based laws
    C. Municipal-based laws
    D. State-based laws

37. Which of the following is used by U.S. corporations (specifically, C Corps) to report income, gains, losses, deductions, and credits, and to determine their tax liability?

    A. IRS Form 1040
    B. IRS Form 1041
    C. IRS Form 1065
    D. IRS Form 1120

38. Pink sheets are to unlisted stocks as _____ are to bonds.

    A. blue sheets
    B. green sheets
    C. white sheets
    D. yellow sheets

39. Which of the following acts promotes efficiency and capital formation in the financial markets, and provides for more effective and less burdensome regulation between states and the Federal Government? It also declared that any offering of a "covered security" is exempt from state registration and review.

   A. Insider Trading and Securities Fraud Enforcement Act of 1988
   B. Uniform Prudent Investors Act of 1994
   C. National Securities Market Improvement Act of 1996
   D. Sarbanes-Oxley Act of 2002

The following information relates to questions 40 – 41.

Stephanie purchased a whole life insurance policy several years ago. She has provided the following information related to the policy.

Face amount	$250,000
Cash value	$87,500
Paid-up additions	$75,000
Cash value of paid-up additions	$50,000
Annual premium	$4,300
Annual dividend	$1,900

40. What is the current surrender value of Stephanie's policy?

   A. $112,500
   B. $137,500
   C. $162,500
   D. $164,400

41. If Stephanie dies, a death benefit of _____ will be paid to her beneficiary.

   A. $250,000
   B. $262,500
   C. $300,000
   D. $325,000

42. An investor purchased a call option for $3.00. The option has a strike price of $37.00, and the stock is currently valued at $36.00. The call option would cost $2.50 if purchased today. Ignoring transaction costs, what is the value of the option?

   A. –$0.50
   B. $0
   C. $1.00
   D. $2.00

43. Which of the following is a graphical representation of a security's average price over a period of time?

A. Moving average
B. Support and resistance average
C. Technical average
D. Trendline average

44. Which of the following is/are correct regarding generation skipping transfers?

(1) A generation skipping transfer may only occur during a transferor's lifetime.
(2) The gift tax annual exclusion may only be used to offset a lifetime generation skipping transfer.

A. (1) only
B. (2) only
C. Both (1) and (2) are correct.
D. Neither (1) or (2) are correct.

45. Which of the following is a private, non-profit organization whose primary purpose is to establish and improve generally accepted accounting principles within the U.S.?

A. FASB
B. FDIC
C. MSRB
D. NSCC

46. When calculating gross domestic product (GDP), all but which of the following variables are paired with the correct description?

A. C = Personal consumption
B. I = Issuance of government bonds
C. G = Government spending
D. E = Net exports

47. Which of the following is the correct method to conducting bottom-up investment analysis?

A. First examine a specific company, then examine a specific industry, then examine a specific economy, then examine the global economy.
B. First examine a specific company, then examine a specific economy, then examine a specific industry, then examine the global economy.
C. First examine the global economy, then examine a specific industry, then examine a specific economy, then examine a specific company.
D. First examine the global economy, then examine a specific economy, then examine a specific industry, then examine a specific company.

48. Which of the following groups may be excluded from participating in an employee stock purchase plan (ESPP)?

    A. Employees working less than 20 hours per week.
    B. Employees with less than 2 years of service.
    C. Officers of the employer.
    D. All of the above are correct.

For questions 49 – 51, match the type of risk with the description that follows. Use only one answer per blank. Answers may be used more than once or not at all.

    A. Business risk
    B. Tax risk
    C. Financial risk
    D. Market risk
    E. Credit risk
    F. Country risk

49. ___ The risk associated with a company's decision to use debt as part of its capital structure.

50. ___ The possibility that a bond issuer will default.

51. ___ The risk inherent in company operations.

52. Which of the following government agencies are responsible for monitoring qualified retirement plan rules and eligibility?

    A. ERISA and the IRS
    B. ERISA and the PBGC
    C. IRS and the Department of Labor
    D. IRS and the PBGC

53. Which of the following is/are correct regarding probate?

    (1) If a person dies testate, his or her property is subject to probate.
    (2) If a person dies intestate, his or her property avoids probate.

    A. (1) only
    B. (2) only
    C. Both (1) and (2) are correct.
    D. Neither (1) or (2) are correct.

54. All but which of the following are characteristics of defined benefit plans?

    A. Employer contributions vary.
    B. Participant benefits vary.
    C. The employer assumes the investment risk.
    D. They favor older employees.

55. Which of the following is correct regarding non-systematic risk?

    A. It includes risks such as tax risk and financial risk.
    B. An investor who owns five growth stocks can reduce non-systematic risk by adding a value stock to her portfolio.
    C. It is the risk associated with a particular security or company.
    D. All of the above are correct.

56. Money in a Coverdell Education Savings Account (ESA) must be used by the time the beneficiary is _____ years of age.

    A. 18
    B. 21
    C. 24
    D. 30

57. Which of the following describes the rate of return calculated by the capital asset pricing model (CAPM)?

    A. The rate of return is not reliable because CAPM fails to take risk into account.
    B. The rate of return can be used in the dividend growth model for valuing common stock.
    C. The rate of return represents the stock market's overall rate of return.
    D. The rate of return is not reliable because CAPM uses beta in its formula.

58. Alpha Inc. reports the following information at its annual shareholder meeting:

Liabilities at year-end	$500,000
Contributed capital at year-end	$100,000
Beginning retained earnings	$150,000
Revenue during the year	$300,000
Expenses during the year	$200,000
Dividends paid during the year	$50,000

    What is the value of Alpha Inc.'s total assets at year-end?

    A. $800,000
    B. $900,000
    C. $1,300,000
    D. $1,350,000

59. Regarding the money supply, which of the following is the formula for M1?

    A. M1 = Savings accounts + Short-term time deposits
    B. M1 = Coins and currency in circulation + Money held in checking accounts
    C. M1 = Long-term time deposits
    D. M1 = Coins and currency in circulation + Short-term time deposits

60. Which of the following is/are correct regarding tax credits?

(1) A refundable tax credit cannot reduce a taxpayer's income tax liability below zero.
(2) A non-refundable tax credit can reduce a taxpayer's income tax liability below zero.

A. (1) only
B. (2) only
C. Both (1) and (2) are correct.
D. Neither (1) or (2) are correct.

For questions 61 – 64, match the legislation with the description that follows. Use only one answer per blank. Answers may be used more than once or not at all.

A. Securities Act of 1933
B. Securities Exchange Act of 1934
C. Investment Company Act of 1940
D. Securities Investor Protection Act of 1970

61. ___ Regulates brokerage firms.

62. ___ Regulates mutual funds.

63. ___ Regulates new securities.

64. ___ Regulates existing securities.

65. Treasury notes, Treasury bonds, and TIPS, whose interest and principal portions have been separated so they may be sold individually, are referred to as which of the following?

A. Treasury GICs
B. Treasury CMOs
C. Treasury STRIPS
D. Treasury UITs

66. Which of the following is/are correct regarding the capital structure of open-end mutual funds?

(1) Open-end mutual funds issue new shares and redeem existing shares from shareholders.
(2) The price an investor pays when buying shares of an open-end mutual fund is based on supply and demand.

A. (1) only
B. (2) only
C. Both (1) and (2) are correct.
D. Neither (1) or (2) are correct.

67. Regulation A permits unregistered public offerings of up to _____ of securities in any 12-month period.

    A. $1 million
    B. $5 million
    C. $10 million
    D. $20 million

68. Which of the following retirement plans require immediate vesting?

    A. Employer contributions to a 401(k) plan.
    B. Employer contributions to a money purchase plan.
    C. Employer contributions to a SEP.
    D. All of the above are correct.

69. How is the net asset value (NAV) of a mutual fund calculated?

    A. NAV = (Total value of investment + Liabilities) ÷ Shares outstanding
    B. NAV = (Total value of investment ÷ Shares outstanding) – Liabilities
    C. NAV = (Total value of investment – Liabilities) ÷ Shares outstanding
    D. NAV = Total value of investment ÷ Shares outstanding

70. According to the anomaly known as the "small-firm effect," _____ companies have been shown to outperform _____ companies on a risk-adjusted basis over a period of many years.

    A. large cap, small cap
    B. mid cap, small cap
    C. small cap, large cap
    D. small cap, mid cap

71. Interest earned on which of the following is a tax preference item for the alternative minimum tax (AMT)?

    A. General obligation bonds
    B. Private activity bonds
    C. Public purpose bonds
    D. Revenue bonds

72. According to the Uniform Securities Act, if the Administrator issues a subpoena and the affected party fails to respond, it is referred to as which of the following?

    A. Adhesion
    B. Contumacy
    C. Estoppel
    D. Rescission

73. A research analyst provides the following economic information for Country X:

Category	Amount ($ billions)
Consumption	11.4
Government spending	3.3
Capital consumption allowance	5.0
Gross private domestic investment	6.2
Imports	2.9
Exports	1.8

What is the gross domestic product (GDP) of Country X?

A. $17.9 billion
B. $18.6 billion
C. $19.8 billion
D. $24.8 billion

74. A corporate insider is defined as a director or senior officer of a company, as well as any person or entity that beneficially owns more than _____ of a company's voting shares.

A. 1%
B. 2%
C. 5%
D. 10%

75. Which of the following securities are backed by the full faith and credit of the U.S. government?

A. Federal Home Loan Mortgage Corporation debentures (Freddie Macs)
B. Federal National Mortgage Association certificates (Fannie Maes)
C. Government National Mortgage Association certificates (Ginnie Maes)
D. Student Loan Marketing Association notes (Sallie Maes)

76. Which of the following investments will provide tax-exempt interest if the proceeds are used to pay for qualifying education expenses?

(1) FNMA funds
(2) Series EE bonds
(3) Treasury bonds
(4) Treasury bills

A. (2) only
B. (1) and (2) only
C. (2), (3), and (4) only
D. All of the above are correct.

77. How are the value of publicly traded stocks and bonds determined for gift and estate tax purposes?

A. The closing price on the date of disposition.
B. The opening price on the date of disposition.
C. The mean between the highest and lowest selling price on the date of disposition.
D. The mean between the highest and lowest selling price on the date prior to the date of disposition.

78. Which of the following is an exchange employee who is in charge of keeping a book of public limit orders on exchanges utilizing the "market-maker" system?

A. Designated market maker
B. Limit order officer
C. Order book official
D. Public order specialist

79. Employer contributions to a defined contribution plan must use either the _____ cliff vesting or _____ graded vesting schedules.

A. 3-year, 6-year
B. 3-year, 7-year
C. 5-year, 6-year
D. 5-year, 7-year

80. Which of the following is a short-term obligation that is issued for temporary financing needs by a municipality?

A. Bond anticipation note
B. Guaranteed investment contract
C. Tax anticipation note
D. Unit investment trust

81. Which of the following is an order to buy a stock at a price above the current market price?

A. Buy stop order
B. Buy limit order
C. Buy market order
D. None of the above are correct.

82. A variable life insurance policy will pay benefits that vary according to which of the following?

A. The flexibility of premiums paid.
B. The value of underlying investments.
C. The variability of the mortality factor.
D. All of the above are correct.

83. Which of the following is correct regarding IAR registration?

   A. Individual registrations can be administered at the state level or federal level, depending on where the RIA firm is registered.
   B. All individual registrations are administered at the federal level, regardless of whether the RIA firm is registered at the SEC or state level.
   C. All individual registrations are administered at the state level, regardless of whether the RIA firm is registered at the SEC or state level.
   D. None of the above are correct.

84. Which of the following estate planning objectives can be accomplished through a will?

   A. Avoiding probate.
   B. Establishing a testamentary trust.
   C. Providing burial wishes.
   D. Providing for decisions during incapacitation.

85. An indenture agreement describes the terms and conditions of a bond, including which of the following?

   A. Call provisions
   B. Description of collateral
   C. How coupon payments are determined
   D. All of the above are correct.

86. Which of the following must be filed for each of the first three fiscal quarters of a company's fiscal year, and includes unaudited financial statements and provides a continuing view of the company's financial position during the year?

   A. Form ADV
   B. Form 8-K
   C. Form 10-K
   D. Form 10-Q

87. Which of the following is an advantage that money purchase plans have over other qualified retirement plans?

   A. Employer contributions can be omitted in certain years and must only be substantial and recurring.
   B. Forfeitures must be used to reduce future employer contributions.
   C. They are easy to explain to employees.
   D. They favor older employees.

88. A trade surplus results from which of the following?

   A. A country having a current account deficit.
   B. A country exporting more than it imports.
   C. A country exporting less than it imports.
   D. None of the above are correct.

89. Eurodollars have which of the following characteristics?

(1) They are foreign denominated deposits in banks located outside the U.S.
(2) They involve deposits made at only European banks.

A. (1) only
B. (2) only
C. Both (1) and (2) are correct.
D. Neither (1) or (2) are correct.

90. According to the principles of behavioral finance, which of the following terms describes an investor's tendency to look for information that supports his or her previously established decision, even if that decision was imprudent? This tendency may explain why investors are slow to sell an underperforming stock.

A. Confirmation bias
B. Expectation bias
C. Hold bias
D. Prospect bias

91. Which of the following is a computerized subscriber service that serves as a vehicle for the fourth market by permitting subscribers to display bids and offers and execute trades electronically?

A. ECN
B. EMMA
C. Instinet
D. NSCC

92. A/An _____ legal opinion means that the bond counsel has no reservations regarding the bond issue, and it is considered the most desirable for investors.

A. binding
B. enforceable
C. qualified
D. unqualified

93. Which of the following is correct regarding certificates of deposit (CDs)?

A. They are short-term securities that may be bought or sold in the open market at a market-determined price.
B. They typically invest in high-quality, short-term investments, such as commercial paper, Treasury bills, and money market funds.
C. They are known as "time deposits."
D. The financial institution typically pays a variable rate of interest for the term of the CD.

94. In any single life private annuity transaction, if the seller outlives his or her actuarial life expectancy, the purchaser will have paid _____ for the property. If the seller does not outlive his or her actuarial life expectancy, the _____ will have made a good financial deal.

   A. too much, purchaser
   B. too much, seller
   C. too little, purchaser
   D. too little, seller

95. The annual report on _____ provides a comprehensive overview of a company's business and financial condition and includes audited financial statements.

   A. Form 6-K
   B. Form 8-K
   C. Form 10-K
   D. Form 10-Q

96. Beta Corporation sold products to customers on April 30, 2017 for a total price of $85,000. Payment is due in 60 days. The total cost of the products was $67,000. What is the net change in Beta Corporation's total assets on April 30, 2017?

   A. $0
   B. $18,000
   C. $67,000
   D. $103,000

97. Which of the following is/are correct regarding cyclical stocks?

   (1) When the economy is growing, demand usually strengthens and cyclical companies are able to make large profits.
   (2) When the economy is declining, cyclical companies are hurt by decreases in demand and are less profitable.

   A. (1) only
   B. (2) only
   C. Both (1) and (2) are correct.
   D. Neither (1) or (2) are correct.

98. Which of the following acts, also known as the Currency and Foreign Transactions Reporting Act, requires financial institutions to assist U.S. government agencies in detecting and preventing money laundering?

   A. Bank Secrecy Act of 1970
   B. Insider Trading and Securities Fraud Enforcement Act of 1988
   C. National Securities Market Improvement Act of 1996
   D. Sarbanes-Oxley Act of 2002

99. Which of the following plans require immediate vesting?

    (1) Money purchase plan
    (2) SEP
    (3) 401(k) plan
    (4) 403(b) plan

    A. (2) only
    B. (1) and (3) only
    C. (2) and (4) only
    D. (1), (2), and (4) only

100. All but which of the following are characteristics of a REIT?

    A. It is a publicly traded open-end investment company.
    B. A mortgage REIT is a specific type of REIT.
    C. A REIT can sell at a premium or discount to its NAV.
    D. All of the above are correct.

101. Which of the following is the typical limit on the term of a loan from a qualified re-
    tirement plan?

    A. 1 year
    B. 2 years
    C. 5 years
    D. 10 years

102. Which of the following refers to taking a loss on a bond and replacing it with a sub-
    stantially different bond to avoid triggering the wash sale rule?

    A. Bond conversion
    B. Bond spread
    C. Bond swap
    D. Bond yield

103. Steve sold his portfolio of ETFs and is now required to pay 15% tax on the gain.
    Which of the following must be true?

    (1) The ETFs were taxed at long-term capital gains rates.
    (2) Steve's marginal tax bracket was less than 25%.
    (3) Steve owned the ETFs for more than one year.
    (4) Steve's marginal tax bracket was 25% or higher.

    A. (1) and (3) only
    B. (3) and (4) only
    C. (1), (2), and (3) only
    D. (1), (3), and (4) only

104. Which of the following will shift the Markowitz efficient frontier to the left?

    A. Taking less risk.
    B. Taking more risk.
    C. Changing the proportion of securities already invested in the portfolio.
    D. Selecting investments with lower coefficients of correlation between them.

105. Which of the following terms refers to a broker using securities in his or her posses-
     sion, but owned by a customer, as collateral to raise a loan to cover a short position?

    A. Recapitalization
    B. Recollateralization
    C. Rehypothecation
    D. Securitization

106. Which of the following is the maximum prison sentence for an insider trading vio-
     lation?

    A. 10 years
    B. 20 years
    C. 30 years
    D. 40 years

107. Which of the following are among the requirements for a valid S Corp election?

    (1) Only one class of stock is permitted.
    (2) There may be no more than 75 shareholders.
    (3) It must be a domestic corporation.
    (4) Shareholders must be U.S. citizens or residents.

    A. (1) and (3) only
    B. (1), (2), and (4) only
    C. (1), (3), and (4) only
    D. (2), (3), and (4) only

108. Which of the following are permitted investments in an IRA?

    A. A mutual fund that invests exclusively in a silver mining stock.
    B. Gold coins minted in the U.S.
    C. A real estate investment trust.
    D. All of the above are correct.

109. (Current assets – Inventory) ÷ Current liabilities = _____

    A. Current ratio
    B. Inventory turnover ratio
    C. Quick ratio
    D. Return on assets

110. To calculate core inflation, which of the following categories are excluded from the calculation?

    A. Food and energy prices
    B. Food and utilities
    C. Healthcare and energy prices
    D. Technology and utilities

111. Investment advisers that have custody of client assets or require prepayment of advisory fees _____ or more in advance, and in excess of _____ for each client, must file an audited balance sheet with the SEC as of the end of the investment adviser's fiscal year.

    A. 6 months, $500
    B. 6 months, $1,000
    C. 12 months, $500
    D. 12 months, $1,000

112. Which of the following mutual fund share classes will charge investors a level load?

    A. Class A shares
    B. Class B shares
    C. Class C shares
    D. Class D shares

113. Investment risk is defined as which of the following?

    A. The chance that an investment's actual return will be greater or less than its expected return.
    B. The chance that an investment's actual return will equal its expected return.
    C. The chance that an investment's actual return will be less than its expected return.
    D. None of the above are correct.

114. All but which of the following are characteristics of sole proprietorships?

    A. They are the simplest form of business entity.
    B. They have no formal legal requirements.
    C. They have a lack of continuity of business life.
    D. They provide limited liability to owners.

115. Which of the following option strategies seeks to maximize an investor's profit when the price of an underlying security decreases in value?

    A. Bear spread
    B. Bull spread
    C. Long straddle
    D. Protective collar

116. Which of the following acts allowed for the establishment of the National Association of Securities Dealers (NASD) and the U.S. domestic over-the-counter markets in securities?

    A. Maloney Act of 1938
    B. Trust Indenture Act of 1939
    C. Investment Company Act of 1940
    D. Uniform Securities Act of 1956

For questions 117 – 119, select the word that best completes the bond relationship provided. Use only one answer per blank. Answers may be used more than once or not at all.

    A. More
    B. Less

117. ___ Lower-coupon bonds are _____ affected by interest rate changes than higher-coupon bonds.

118. ___ The shorter a bond's term to maturity, the _____ its potential for relative price fluctuation.

119. ___ Long-term bonds are _____ affected by interest rate changes than short-term bonds.

120. Which of the following are correct regarding qualified personal residence trusts (QPRTs)?

    (1) A QPRT is ideal for a single parent in his 30s or 40s.
    (2) A QPRT is generally appropriate for vacation homes valued at over $1,000,000.
    (3) After the trust term ends, the house reverts back to the grantor.
    (4) The grantor will have a taxable gift upon the creation of a QPRT.

    A. (1) and (2) only
    B. (2) and (3) only
    C. (2) and (4) only
    D. (1), (3), and (4) only

121. Which of the following sections of the tax code allows individuals to make withdrawals before age 59 ½ from certain retirement accounts without penalty, as long as the SEPP (substantially equal periodic payment) regulation is met?

    A. Rule 67(e)
    B. Rule 72(t)
    C. Rule 83(b)
    D. Rule 501(r)

122. Dawn contributed $12,000 to a qualified retirement plan several years ago. The account balance is now $14,500. If Dawn takes a lump sum distribution, she will owe:

A. long-term capital gains tax on $2,500.
B. long-term capital gains tax on $14,500.
C. ordinary income tax on $2,500.
D. ordinary income tax on $14,500.

123. Which of the following is required for an individual to open a health savings account (HSA)?

A. The individual must have a high-deductible health plan (HDHP).
B. The individual must have a low-deductible health plan (LDHP).
C. The individual must have a flexible spending account (FSA).
D. None of the above are required to open a health savings account.

124. Which of the following statements about property held as tenancy by entirety are correct?

(1) The property automatically passes to the surviving co-tenant when one tenant dies.
(2) It is an interest in property that can be held only by spouses.
(3) It can be held by non-spouse business partners in an LLC.
(4) In most states, it is not severable by an individual tenant.

A. (1) and (2) only
B. (2) and (4) only
C. (1), (2), and (3) only
D. (1), (2), and (4) only

125. Kappa Inc. provides the following information at its annual shareholder meeting:

Gross income	$2,300,000
Net income	$950,000
Number of shares outstanding	250,000
Price per share	$9.10
Average total book value of equity	$3,260,000
Total liabilities	$2,980,000

What is Kappa Inc.'s return on equity (ROE)?

A. 27.72%
B. 29.14%
C. 31.88%
D. 33.59%

For questions 126 – 129, match the hedging technique with the description that follows. Use only one answer per blank. Answers may be used more than once or not at all.

A. Collar
B. Spread
C. Straddle
D. Protective put

126. ___ Purchasing a call option and selling a call option on the same stock at the same time.

127. ___ Purchasing a put option and selling a call option on the same stock at the same time.

128. ___ Purchasing a put option while holding shares of the underlying stock from a previous purchase.

129. ___ Purchasing a call option and a put option on the same stock at the same time.

130. Which of the following is the official repository for information on virtually all municipal bonds, and provides free access to official disclosures, trade data, and other information about the municipal securities market?

A. EMMA
B. FAST
C. MSRB
D. TRACE

ANSWER KEY

1. C
A rights offering is an offering of shares to existing stockholders on a pro-rata basis.

2. D
Open market operations is a tool used by the Federal Reserve to implement monetary policy. It is conducted by the Trading Desk at the Federal Reserve Bank of New York, and the authority to conduct open market operations is found in Section 14 of the Federal Reserve Act.

3. A
With REMICs (real estate mortgage investment conduits), investors receive a specified cash flow from the underlying mortgages. They combine the predictable cash flow of a bond with the high yield of a mortgage-backed security. REMICs are self-liquidating and have a limited life that terminates when the underlying mortgages are repaid.

4. D
A sell stop order is an order to sell a stock at a price below the current market price.

5. D
As a cyber security measure, broker-dealers should utilize a two-step verification process, which means that each time a user attempts to log into an investment account through an unrecognized device, the investment firm will send a unique code to the user via email or text message. Before the user can access the account, he or she must enter the code and password.

6. C
Because Justin is an active participant in an employer-sponsored retirement plan, he is subject to an AGI phaseout of $63,000 to $73,000 in 2018. Because his income is above the phaseout range, he is not eligible to make a deductible IRA contribution. His AGI is too high to contribute to a Roth IRA, as well. The Roth IRA AGI phaseout is $120,000 to $135,000 in 2018.

7. A
When an investment company puts home mortgages or other loans into a pool and then sells securities representing shares of the pool, the securities sold are referred to as asset-backed securities.

8. A
If the yield curve is flattening, then the spread between yields of short-term and long-term bonds is decreasing.

9. B
The preliminary prospectus is also referred to as a "red herring."

10. D
Selling a naked call will expose an investor to the greatest amount of risk.

11. B
Monthly interest rate = 3.2% ÷ 3 months = 1.07%
Annual interest rate = 3.2% × 4 quarters = 12.80%

12. C
The Federal Reserve supervises and regulates banks, and operates and oversees the U.S. payment system. It derives its authority from Congress.

13. B
An income statement is also referred to as a statement of financial performance, statement of operations, and statement of profit or loss. A statement of financial position is another name for a balance sheet.

14. C
Real return is an investment's rate of return after adjusting for inflation. Nominal return is an investment's rate of return without adjusting for inflation.

15. A
According to the arbitrage pricing theory, security prices in different markets will not differ for any significant period of time.

16. B
In order to obtain a viatical settlement, the insured must be terminally ill and must have owned the policy for at least two years. The current beneficiary of the policy must sign a release or waiver, and the insured must sign a release allowing the viatical settlement provider access to his or her medical records.

17. A
A qualified domestic trust (QDOT) allows property to pass to a non-U.S. citizen spouse and still qualify for the marital deduction. In order for a QDOT to be valid, there must be at least one trustee who is a U.S. citizen or a qualifying domestic corporation.

18. D
The primary issuers of individual bonds are local government, state government, U.S. government, an agency of the U.S. government, and corporations.

19. C
Taxes owed from tax deduction = ($80,000 – $8,000) × 0.25 = $18,000

20. B
Taxes owed from tax credit = ($80,000 × 0.25) – $4,000 = $16,000

21. A
Step 1: Taxes owed from tax deduction = ($80,000 – $8,000) × 0.25 = $18,000
Step 2: Equivalent tax credit = ($80,000 × 0.25) – $18,000 = $2,000

22. A
Mutual fund turnover rate = Gross proceeds from sale of securities ÷ NAV

23. B
Higher inflation = higher interest rates = lower bond values

24. C
If a wash sale occurs, no loss deduction is allowed, and the amount of the disallowed loss is added to the cost basis of the newly acquired shares.

25. D
Regardless of income, participating in a 457 plan does not affect the deductibility of Lisa's IRA contribution. Participating in a 401(k) or 403(b) would eliminate Lisa's ability to deduct her IRA contribution because her income is over the threshold.

26. C
6 quarters – 3 quarters = 3 quarters
An economic depression is defined as a decline in real GDP for 6 or more consecutive quarters.

27. B
A Chinese wall is the ethical barrier that is required between different divisions of a financial institution to avoid conflicts of interest.

28. D
Preferred stock that does not have to pay missed dividends is considered noncumulative.

29. A
Securities Act Rule 145 addresses the registration and resale requirements for securities issued in a merger, consolidation, acquisition of assets, or reclassification of securities.

30. C
The "cooling-off period," which transpires between the filing of a new issue's prospectus and the actual offering of the issue, must be a minimum of 20 days.

31. C
Brady bonds are typically issued by Latin American countries.

32. B
Expansionary policy is characterized by decreasing taxes, increasing public spending, and increasing government borrowing.

33. D
In order to maintain a SIMPLE plan, an employer may not have more than 100 employees.

34. C
An investment-grade bond is one that is rated BBB- or higher by the Standard & Poor's bond rating service. A high-yield bond is rated BB+ or lower by Standard & Poor's.

35. B
A planned amortization class (PAC) bond has the most stable cash flows and the lowest prepayment risk of any class of CMO (collateralized mortgage obligation).

36. D
Blue sky laws are classified as state-based laws.

37. D
IRS Form 1120 is used by U.S. corporations (specifically, C Corps) to report their income, gains, losses, deductions, and credits, and to determine their tax liability.

38. D
Pink sheets are to unlisted stocks as yellow sheets are to bonds.

39. C
The National Securities Market Improvement Act of 1996 promotes efficiency and capital formation in the financial markets, and provides for more effective and less burdensome regulation between states and the Federal Government. It also declared that any offering of a "covered security" (as defined within the Act) is exempt from state registration and review.

40. B
Surrender value = $87,500 + $50,000 = $137,500

41. D
Death benefit = $250,000 + $75,000 = $325,000

42. B
The call option is out-of-the-money because the strike price ($37.00) exceeds the market price ($36.00). Therefore, the value of the option is $0.

43. A
The moving average is a graphical representation of a security's average price over a period of time.

44. B
A generation skipping transfer may occur during the transferor's lifetime or at the transferor's death. The gift tax annual exclusion may only be used to offset a lifetime generation skipping transfer.

45. A
The FASB (Financial Accounting Standards Board) is a private, non-profit organization whose primary purpose is to establish and improve generally accepted accounting principles within the U.S.

46. B
Gross Domestic Product (GDP) = C + I + G + E
C = Personal consumption
I = Gross private domestic investment
G = Government spending
E = Net exports

47. A

To conduct bottom-up investment analysis, first examine a specific company, then examine a specific industry, then examine a specific economy, then examine the global economy.

48. D

All of the groups listed may be excluded from participating in an employee stock purchase plan (ESPP). These include employees working less than 20 hours per week, employees with less than 2 years of service, and officers of the employer.

49. C

Financial risk is the risk associated with a company's decision to use debt as part of its capital structure.

50. E

Credit risk is the possibility that a bond issuer will default.

51. A

Business risk is the risk inherent in company operations.

52. C

The two government agencies responsible for monitoring qualified retirement plan rules and eligibility are the IRS and the Department of Labor.

53. A

If a person dies testate or intestate, his or her property will be subject to probate.

54. B

In a defined benefit plan, employer contributions can vary but participant benefits are fixed. The employer assumes the investment risk, and they tend to favor older employees.

55. D

Non-systematic risk is the risk associated with a particular security or company. It includes risks such as tax risk and financial risk. An investor who owns five growth stocks can reduce non-systematic risk by adding a value stock to her portfolio.

56. D

Money in a Coverdell Education Savings Account (ESA) must be used by the time the beneficiary is 30 years of age.

57. B

The capital asset pricing model (CAPM) calculates the required rate of return for a stock based on its beta and the stock market's overall rate of return. That rate of return can then be used in the dividend growth model to value common stock.

58. A

Total assets = Liabilities at year-end + Contributed capital at year-end + Beginning retained earnings + Revenues – Expenses – Dividends

Total assets = $500,000 + $100,000 + $150,000 + 300,000 – $200,000 – $50,000

Total assets = $800,000

59. B
M1 = Coins and currency in circulation + Money held in checking accounts

60. D
A refundable tax credit can reduce a taxpayer's income tax liability below zero. A non-refundable tax credit cannot reduce a taxpayer's income tax liability below zero.

61. D
The Securities Investor Protection Act of 1970 regulates brokerage firms.

62. C
The Investment Company Act of 1940 regulates mutual funds.

63. A
The Securities Act of 1933 regulates new securities.

64. B
The Securities Exchange Act of 1934 regulates existing securities.

65. C
Treasury notes, Treasury bonds, and TIPS, whose interest and principal portions have been separated so they may be sold individually, are referred to as Treasury STRIPS.

66. A
Open-end mutual funds issue new shares and redeem existing shares from shareholders. The price an investor pays when buying shares of an open-end mutual fund is based on the fund's net asset value (NAV).

67. B
Regulation A permits unregistered public offerings of up to $5 million of securities in any 12-month period.

68. C
Employer contributions to a SEP require immediate vesting. A 401(k) plan and money purchase plan may use alternate vesting schedules for employer contributions.

69. C
NAV = (Total value of investment – Liabilities) ÷ Shares outstanding

70. C
According to the anomaly known as the small-firm effect, small cap companies have been shown to outperform large cap companies on a risk-adjusted basis over a period of many years.

71. B
Interest earned on private activity bonds is a tax preference item for alternative minimum tax (AMT).

72. B
According to the Uniform Securities Act, if the Administrator issues a subpoena and the affected party fails to respond, it is referred to as contumacy.

73. C
GDP = C + I + G + (X – M)
GDP = $11.4 + $6.2 + $3.3 + ($1.8 – $2.9) = $19.8 billion

74. D
A corporate insider is defined as a director or senior officer of a company, as well as any person or entity that beneficially owns more than 10% of a company's voting shares.

75. C
Only Government National Mortgage Association certificates (Ginnie Maes) are backed by the full faith and credit of the U.S. government.

76. A
Series EE bonds provide tax-exempt interest if the proceeds are used to pay for qualifying education expenses.

77. C
The value of publicly traded stocks and bonds is the mean between the highest and lowest quoted selling price on the date of disposition for gift and estate tax purposes.

78. C
An order book official (OBO) is an exchange employee who is in charge of keeping a book of public limit orders on exchanges utilizing the "market-maker" system.

79. A
Employer contributions to a defined contribution plan must use either the 3-year cliff vesting or 6-year graded vesting schedules.

80. A
A bond anticipation note (BAN) is a short-term obligation that is issued for temporary financing needs by a municipality.

81. A
A buy stop order is an order to buy a stock at a price above the current market price.

82. B
A variable life insurance policy will pay benefits that vary according to the value of the underlying investments.

83. C
Regarding IAR registration, all individual registrations are administered at the state level, regardless of whether the RIA firm is registered at the SEC or state level.

84. B
Wills do not avoid probate. Planning for incapacity is addressed through powers of attorney, not through the will. The will is often read after the decedent's funeral, therefore burial wishes should not be included. A will can be used to establish a testamentary trust.

85. D
An indenture agreement describes the terms and conditions of a bond, including call provisions, description of collateral, and how coupon payments are determined.

86. D
Form 10-Q must be filed for each of the first three fiscal quarters of a company's fiscal year. It includes unaudited financial statements and provides a continuing view of the company's financial position during the year.

87. C
Money purchase plans are easy to explain to employees because contributions are based on a flat percentage of compensation. Money purchase plans tend to favor younger employees, and forfeitures can be reallocated to remaining employees. Contributions cannot be omitted in certain years. The "substantial and recurring" rule only applies to profit sharing plans.

88. B
A trade surplus results from a country exporting more than it imports.

89. D
Eurodollars are U.S. dollar denominated deposits in banks located outside the U.S. They do not involve deposits at only European banks.

90. A
Confirmation bias describes an investor's tendency to look for information that supports his or her previously established decision, even if that decision was imprudent. It may explain why investors are slow to sell an underperforming stock.

91. C
The Instinet is a computerized subscriber service that serves as a vehicle for the fourth market by permitting subscribers to display bids and offers and execute trades electronically.

92. D
An unqualified legal opinion means that the bond counsel has no reservations regarding the bond issue, and it is considered the most desirable for investors.

93. C
Certificates of deposit (CDs) are known as "time deposits." They are deposits made with a bank for a specified period of time.

94. A
In any single life private annuity transaction, if the seller outlives his or her actuarial life expectancy, the purchaser will have paid too much for the property. If the seller does not outlive his or her actuarial life expectancy, the purchaser will have made a good financial deal.

95. C
The annual report on Form 10-K provides a comprehensive overview of a company's business and financial condition and includes audited financial statements.

96. B

$85,000 - $67,000 = $18,000.

Accounts receivable (an asset) increases by $85,000. The balance in inventory (an asset) decreases by $67,000. The net increase in assets is $18,000.

97. C

Cyclical stocks tend to prosper in growing and expanding economies, and do poorly during down business cycles.

98. A

The Bank Secrecy Act of 1970, also known as the Currency and Foreign Transactions Reporting Act, requires financial institutions to assist U.S. government agencies in detecting and preventing money laundering.

99. A

A SEP requires immediate vesting. A money purchase plan, 401(k) plan, and 403(b) plan may use alternate vesting schedules.

100. A

REITs are publicly traded closed-end investment companies that can sell at a premium or discount to its NAV. A mortgage REIT is a specific type of REIT.

101. C

The typical limit on the term of a loan from a qualified retirement plan is 5 years.

102. C

A bond swap refers to taking a loss on a bond and replacing it with a substantially different bond to avoid triggering the wash sale rule.

103. D

For the 15% capital gains rate to apply, Steve must be in a marginal tax bracket of 25% or higher. To qualify for long-term capital gains, assets must be held for more than one year.

104. D

Taking more or less risk will move the investor's position along the efficient frontier, but will not shift it. The same is true of changing the proportion of securities already invested in the portfolio. However, by selecting investments with lower coefficients of correlation, the risk will be reduced and the efficient frontier will shift upward and to the left.

105. C

Rehypothecation refers to a broker using securities in his or her possession, but owned by a customer, as collateral to raise a loan to cover a short position.

106. B

The maximum prison sentence for an insider trading violation is 20 years.

107. C

An S Corp must be a domestic corporation and may have up to 100 shareholders. All shareholders must be U.S. citizens or residents. Only one class of stock is permitted with an S Corp.

108. D
All of the items listed are permitted investments in an IRA. These include a mutual fund that invests exclusively in a silver mining stock, gold coins minted in the U.S., and a real estate investment trust (REIT).

109. C
(Current assets – Inventory) ÷ Current liabilities = Quick ratio

110. A
To calculate core inflation, food and energy prices are excluded from the calculation.

111. A
Investment advisers that have custody of client assets or require prepayment of advisory fees 6 months or more in advance, and in excess of $500 for each client, must file an audited balance sheet with the SEC as of the end of the investment adviser's fiscal year.

112. C
Class C mutual fund shares charge a level load.

113. C
Investment risk is the chance that an investment's actual return will be less than its expected return.

114. D
Sole proprietorships are the simplest form of business entity, and they have no formal legal requirements. They have a lack of continuity of business life and provide unlimited liability to owners.

115. A
A bear spread seeks to maximize an investor's profit when the price of an underlying security decreases in value.

116. A
The Maloney Act of 1938 allowed for the establishment of the National Association of Securities Dealers (NASD) and the U.S. domestic over-the-counter markets in securities.

117. A
Lower-coupon bonds are more affected by interest rate changes than higher-coupon bonds. Lower-coupon bonds have more price volatility.

118. B
The shorter a bond's term to maturity, the less its potential for relative price fluctuation. Long-term bonds have more price volatility.

119. A
Long-term bonds are more affected by interest rate changes than short-term bonds. Long-term bonds have more price volatility.

120. C
Qualified personal residence trusts (QPRTs) are commonly used for vacation homes, and homes valued over $1,000,000. The grantor will have a taxable gift upon the creation of a QPRT.

121. B
Rule 72(t) of the tax code allows individuals to make withdrawals before age 59 ½ from certain retirement accounts without penalty, as long as the SEPP (substantially equal periodic payment) regulation is met.

122. D
Because Dawn contributed to a qualified retirement plan, the entire amount that she withdraws will be taxed as ordinary income.

123. A
To open a health savings account (HSA), an individual must have a high-deductible health plan (HDHP).

124. D
Tenancy by entirety is a form of joint tenancy allowed for married couples. It is severable only by both spouses, and the property automatically passes to the surviving spouse when the first spouse dies.

125. B
$ROE_t = NI_t \div \text{Average } BVE_t$
$ROE_t = \$950,000 \div \$3,260,000 = 0.2914 = 29.14\%$

126. B
A spread is the simultaneous purchase of one option and the sale of another option on the same side or position within the market. For example, purchasing a call option and selling a call option on the same stock at the same time is a spread.

127. A
A collar is a technique used to protect an investor's gain in a long position of stock. Specifically, an investor purchases a put option to protect against a decline in the value of an underlying stock, and sells a call option to generate premium income to cover the cost of the put option premium.

128. D
In a protective put, an investor purchases a put option while holding shares of an underlying stock from a previous purchase.

129. C
A straddle is the simultaneous purchase of a call option and a put option on the same stock at the same time.

130. A
EMMA (Electronic Municipal Market Access System) is the official repository for information on virtually all municipal bonds, and provides free access to official disclosures, trade data, and other information about the municipal securities market.

PRACTICE EXAM 6

QUESTIONS

1. Colin would like to offer a retirement plan to the employees at his small retail store. He's considering either a SIMPLE or a SEP. Which of the following is a possible disadvantage to Colin if he selects a SEP?

   A. A SEP must provide for a qualified preretirement survivor annuity (QPSA).
   B. Loans from a SEP are only permitted under limited circumstances.
   C. Employer contributions to a SEP are subject to FICA/FUTA withholding.
   D. An employee age 21 or older, earning $6.50 per hour, who works as few as two hours per week and who has done so for three years is eligible to participate in a SEP.

2. Which of the following is/are correct regarding dividends paid by growth stocks and value stocks?

   (1) Because they are growing and expanding, growth stocks typically do not pay large dividends.
   (2) Most of the earnings generated from value stocks are reinvested back into the company.

   A. (1) only
   B. (2) only
   C. Both (1) and (2) are correct.
   D. Neither (1) or (2) are correct.

3. Edward purchased 100 shares of Theta stock for $55 per share. At the end of two years, he sold the shares for $60 per share. In the first year, the stock did not pay a dividend. In the second year, the stock paid a $4 dividend. What was the holding period return of Edward's investment?

   A. 10.09%
   B. 13.21%
   C. 16.36%
   D. 19.18%

4. All but which of the following are correct regarding the process of underwriting an insurance policy?

   A. Underwriting refers to the process of selecting, classifying, and pricing applicants for insurance.
   B. The underwriter is the individual who decides to accept or reject an application, and under what conditions the policy may be issued.
   C. One of the objectives of underwriting is to generate revenue while at the same time limiting the insurance company's assumed risk.
   D. Restrictive underwriting typically results in higher overall claims made by policyholders.

5. According to modern portfolio theory, an investor's optimal portfolio is located at the point of tangency of the investor's _____ and the _____ of available investment assets.

A. indifference curve, efficient frontier
B. marginal utility curve, efficient frontier
C. marginal utility curve, indifference curve
D. optimal portfolio, efficient frontier

6. Which of the following is more beneficial to a taxpayer in a 28% tax bracket, a $4,000 deduction or a $1,000 credit?

A. The credit will benefit the taxpayer by an additional $120.
B. The deduction will benefit the taxpayer by an additional $120.
C. The deduction will benefit the taxpayer by an additional $300.
D. The deduction and credit will benefit the taxpayer by the same amount.

7. Which of the following allow investors to aggregate their own holdings as well as the holdings of certain related parties, such as spouses and children, toward achieving the investment thresholds at which breakpoint discounts become available?

A. Rights of accumulation
B. Rights of conversion
C. Rights of deferment
D. Rights of indenture

8. A currency transaction report (CTR) must be filed by U.S. financial institutions for each deposit, withdrawal, exchange of currency, or other payment to the institution which involves a transaction in currency of more than:

A. $5,000.
B. $10,000.
C. $25,000.
D. $50,000.

9. Which of the following is/are correct regarding simple and complex trusts?

(1) A simple trust is required to pay out all of its income annually to trust beneficiaries and cannot distribute trust principal.
(2) A complex trust may accumulate income or make distributions from trust principal.

A. (1) only
B. (2) only
C. Both (1) and (2) are correct.
D. Neither (1) or (2) are correct.

For questions 10 – 15, match the type of risk with the description that follows. Use only one answer per blank. Answers may be used more than once or not at all.

    A. Systematic risk
    B. Unsystematic risk

10. ___ Purchasing power risk

11. ___ Business risk

12. ___ Market risk

13. ___ Financial risk

14. ___ Interest rate risk

15. ___ Exchange rate risk

16. Which of the following is the maximum criminal fine for an individual who commits an insider trading violation?

    A. $1 million
    B. $5 million
    C. $10 million
    D. $15 million

17. If $1 is deposited in an interest-bearing account earning 8.5% annually, and the interest is not withdrawn, the account value at the end of 3 years will be:

    A. $1.18.
    B. $1.28.
    C. $1.39.
    D. $1.50.

18. Buying a _____ and selling a _____ are both bullish strategies.

    A. call, call
    B. call, put
    C. put, call
    D. put, put

19. According to the Uniform Securities Act, which of the following are classified as securities?

    A. Collectibles
    B. Fixed annuities
    C. Warrants
    D. Whole life insurance policies

20. Which of the following is a weighted index of prices measured at the wholesale level?

    A. CPI
    B. GNP
    C. NNI
    D. PPI

21. Distributions from a 401(k) plan following separation from service after age _____ are not subject to the _____ premature distribution penalty.

    A. 50, 10%
    B. 50, 15%
    C. 55, 10%
    D. 55, 15%

22. All but which of the following are characteristics of defined benefit plans?

    A. Actuarial calculations are required.
    B. The employee assumes the investment risk.
    C. They favor older employees.
    D. None of the above are correct.

23. Which of the following are short-term, fixed-income securities that may be bought or sold in the open market at a market-determined price?

    A. ADRs
    B. Call options
    C. Eurodollars
    D. Negotiable CDs

24. Epsilon Inc. provides the following information in its annual report (in millions):

Shareholders' equity	$57,500
Fixed assets	$48,200
Total debt	$44,100
Revenue	$66,900
Expenses	$53,800

What is Epsilon Inc.'s debt-to-capital ratio?

    A. 43.4%
    B. 57.3%
    C. 65.9%
    D. 70.8%

25. ERISA Section 404(c) offers a/an _____ for retirement plan fiduciaries to not be liable for investment losses suffered by plan participants who self-direct their investments.

    A. excise tax
    B. penalty
    C. safe harbor
    D. tax shelter

26. Viatical payments to a terminally ill insured are _____ if he or she has a life expectancy of _____.

    A. non-taxable, two years or less
    B. non-taxable, three years or more
    C. taxable, two years or less
    D. taxable, three years or more

27. The U.S. government conducts _____ policy through government spending and taxation.

    A. fiscal
    B. fiscal and monetary
    C. open market
    D. monetary

28. A health savings account (HSA) can be used to pay for which of the following medical expenses incurred by the account owner?

    A. Deductibles
    B. Copayments
    C. Coinsurance
    D. All of the above

29. Which of the following are indexed to the rate of inflation as measured by the CPI?

    A. REITs
    B. REMICs
    C. TIPS
    D. UITs

30. All but which of the following are typically included in ADV Part 1?

    A. Affiliations
    B. Company ownership
    C. Disciplinary history
    D. Fee schedule

31. Which of the following is/are correct regarding the regulation of insurance companies and broker-dealers?

    (1) Insurance company regulation occurs primarily at the state level.
    (2) Broker-dealer regulation occurs primarily at the state level.

    A. (1) only
    B. (2) only
    C. Both (1) and (2) are correct.
    D. Neither (1) or (2) are correct.

32. Which of the following is correct regarding the taxation of Treasury STRIPS?

    A. Tax must be paid on accrued interest each year even though no interest is received by the investor.
    B. Tax is not paid on accrued interest each year because no interest is received by the investor.
    C. Tax must be paid at maturity only.
    D. Treasury STRIPS are not taxed.

33. Prices for goods and services will _____ when their demand exceeds their supply.

    A. deflate
    B. inflate
    C. stagflate
    D. remain unchanged

34. All but which of the following are permitted to establish a 403(b) plan for its employees?

    A. Federal government
    B. Private school
    C. Public school
    D. State government

35. All but which of the following are types of REITs?

    A. Equity REIT
    B. Hybrid REIT
    C. Mortgage REIT
    D. All of the above are correct.

36. A "penny stock" is an equity security that trades below:

    A. $0.05.
    B. $0.50.
    C. $1.00.
    D. $5.00.

37. What is the maximum contribution a donor can make in a single year to a 529 plan if the gift tax annual exclusion is $15,000? Assume the donor has not made previous contributions to a 529 plan.

    A. $15,000
    B. $30,000
    C. $75,000
    D. $105,000

38. Pete, an elderly business owner, is interested in establishing a retirement plan that will provide the greatest retirement benefit to himself. Which of the following plans should Pete select?

    A. Defined benefit plan
    B. Defined contribution plan
    C. Money purchase plan
    D. 401(k) plan

39. Which of the following is/are correct regarding open-end mutual funds?

    (1) Open-end mutual funds sell at their net asset value (NAV).
    (2) Open-end mutual funds have a fixed capital structure.

    A. (1) only
    B. (2) only
    C. Both (1) and (2) are correct.
    D. Neither (1) or (2) are correct.

40. According to Rule 206(4)-5 adopted by the SEC under the Investment Advisers Act of 1940, investment advisers are prohibited from providing advisory services for compensation to a government entity client for _____ after the adviser has made a contribution to certain elected officials or candidates.

    A. 1 year
    B. 2 years
    C. 3 years
    D. 5 years

41. Which of the following is not considered a skip person for generation-skipping transfer tax (GSTT) purposes?

    (1) The transferor's spouse or former spouse, regardless of age.
    (2) A grandchild of the transferor, if the transferor's child is deceased at the time of transfer.

    A. (1) only
    B. (2) only
    C. Both (1) and (2) are correct.
    D. Neither (1) or (2) are correct.

For questions 42 – 46, match each security description with the term that follows. Use only one answer per blank. Answers may be used more than once or not at all.

   A. Freely traded in the secondary markets; yield and term are determined at the time of purchase.
   B. Pay a fixed rate of interest every six months until maturity; issued in terms of ten years or more.
   C. Can be redeemed at any time without penalty; objective is to earn interest for shareholders.
   D. Unsecured promissory note issued by corporations with a fixed maturity of up to 270 days.
   E. Intended to be held until maturity, but can be redeemed prior to maturity for a penalty.
   F. Dividends are declared in local currencies and paid in U.S. dollars.

42. ___ Money market funds

43. ___ Certificate of deposit

44. ___ Commercial paper

45. ___ Treasury bonds

46. ___ American Depository Receipts

47. Which of the following is the first prospectus released for a new issue, and is intended to solicit indications of interest? It does not contain the new issue's price, and it is subject to change.

   A. Pink sheet
   B. Red herring
   C. Shelf registration
   D. Tombstone ad

48. Which of the following is/are correct regarding the early withdrawal penalty from a SIMPLE 401(k)?

   (1) Early withdrawals are subject to a 25% penalty if the withdrawals are made during the first two years of plan participation.
   (2) After the initial two-year period, early withdrawals from a SIMPLE 401(k) are subject to a 15% penalty.

   A. (1) only
   B. (2) only
   C. Both (1) and (2) are correct.
   D. Neither (1) or (2) are correct.

49. Which of the following is a measure of the timing of cash flows (i.e., the interest payments and the principal repayment) to be received from a fixed income security? It's used to assess price volatility for changes in interest rates and the reinvestment risk associated with a portfolio.

    A. Convexity
    B. Duration
    C. Term
    D. Yield

50. During a recent recession, your client, Charles, purchased high-yield corporate bonds that now face minimal default risk. However, he's now concerned that the various corporations may decide to call their bonds. You tell Charles that corporations are likely to call their bonds when:

    A. interest rates are expected to drop.
    B. the bonds are selling at a significant premium.
    C. inflation is expected to rise.
    D. interest rates have declined.

51. If an investor's brokerage firm goes out of business and is a member of the SIPC, then the investor's cash and securities held by the firm may be protected up to _____, including a _____ limit for cash.

    A. $500,000, $250,000
    B. $500,000, $500,000
    C. $1,000,000, $250,000
    D. $1,000,000, $500,000

52. Which of the following is/are correct regarding a flat yield curve?

    (1) It generally indicates an economic slowdown.
    (2) It occurs when there is little difference between short-term and long-term yields for debt instruments of the same credit quality.

    A. (1) only
    B. (2) only
    C. Both (1) and (2) are correct.
    D. Neither (1) or (2) are correct.

53. Which of the following refers to the inverse relationship between bond prices and an investor's required rate of return?

    A. Credit risk
    B. Interest rate risk
    C. Liquidity risk
    D. Reinvestment risk

54. Which of the following is the maximum criminal fine for a non-natural person (such as an entity whose securities are publicly traded) who commits an insider trading violation?

    A. $5 million
    B. $10 million
    C. $25 million
    D. $50 million

55. Which of the following regulations sets out certain requirements for lenders, other than securities brokers and dealers, who extend credit secured by margin stock?

    A. Regulation S
    B. Regulation T
    C. Regulation U
    D. Regulation W

56. According to the anomaly known as the P/E effect, _____ P/E stocks appear to out-perform _____ P/E stocks over annual periods after being adjusted for risk and size.

    A. average, low
    B. high, average
    C. high, low
    D. low, high

57. Which of the following calculates the required amount of an employer's annual contribution to a defined benefit plan to ensure that current and future plan benefits are available to the participants?

    A. Administrator
    B. Actuary
    C. Broker
    D. Enrolled agent

58. Which of the following are liquidity ratios?

    (1) Current ratio
    (2) Debt-to-equity ratio
    (3) Quick ratio
    (4) Fixed asset turnover ratio

    A. (1) and (2) only
    B. (1) and (3) only
    C. (1), (2), and (4) only
    D. (2), (3), and (4) only

59. Which of the following acts created the SEC and empowered it with broad authority over all aspects of the securities industry?

   A. Securities Act of 1933
   B. Securities Exchange Act of 1934
   C. Investment Advisers Act of 1940
   D. Investment Company Act of 1940

60. Earnings before interest and taxes (EBIT) ÷ Annual sales = _____

   A. Average collection period
   B. Net profit margin
   C. Operating profit margin
   D. Quick ratio

61. When a person dies leaving a will, he or she is said to die _____. When a person dies without leaving a will, he or she dies _____.

   A. testate, intestate
   B. intestate, testate
   C. testate, nuncupative
   D. intestate, nuncupative

62. All but which of the following are potential benefits of a bond swap?

   A. It can reduce an investor's tax liability.
   B. It can provide a higher rate of return.
   C. It can provide investment diversification.
   D. All of the above are correct.

63. If a corporation is required to pay unpaid dividends from prior years before paying a dividend to common stockholders, the stock is considered to be:

   A. accumulated preferred stock.
   B. convertible stock.
   C. cumulative preferred stock.
   D. preferred stock.

64. To be considered an accredited investor, earned income must exceed _____ (or _____ together with a spouse) in each of the prior two years, and must be reasonably expected to occur for the current year.

   A. $200,000, $300,000
   B. $300,000, $400,000
   C. $400,000, $500,000
   D. $500,000, $600,000

65. Assume that an investor's portfolio has a return of 15%, a standard deviation of 7%, and a beta of 2.0. If the risk-free rate of return is 4%, what is the portfolio's Sharpe ratio?

 A. 0.06
 B. 1.57
 C. 1.85
 D. 2.14

66. Profit sharing plans have which of the following characteristics?

 A. They favor older employees.
 B. They can be invested entirely in company stock.
 C. They are a type of defined contribution pension plan.
 D. The minimum funding standard requires the employer to make an annual contribution.

67. Which of the following acts provides the tools required to intercept and obstruct terrorism? Title III of this act is intended to facilitate the prevention, detection, and prosecution of international money laundering and the financing of terrorism.

 A. Insider Trading and Securities Fraud Enforcement Act of 1988
 B. Patriot Act of 2001
 C. Sarbanes-Oxley Act of 2002
 D. Dodd-Frank Wall Street Reform and Consumer Protection Act of 2010

68. Tom and Lynn Smith have lived in a community property state all their married lives. They own a house that is registered only in Lynn's name. If she dies, what will happen to the house?

 A. The house will pass automatically to Tom.
 B. The house will pass automatically to Lynn's closest family member.
 C. The house will pass through Lynn's will, and the entire house will go to Tom.
 D. Lynn's half of the house will pass by will. Tom already owns half under community property laws.

69. Nicholas, age 85, is tax sensitive and wants to pay the least amount of estate taxes at death. Which of the following techniques can he potentially use to reduce his gross estate, and therefore, reduce his estate taxes?

 (1) Living trust
 (2) Family limited partnership
 (3) QPRT
 (4) Totten trust

 A. (1) and (2) only
 B. (2) and (3) only
 C. (2) and (4) only
 D. (1), (3), and (4) only

70. Which of the following describes the difference between a 401(k) plan and a 403(b) plan?

    A. A 401(k) plan is a qualified plan, and a 403(b) plan is not a qualified plan.
    B. A 403(b) plan is a qualified plan, and a 401(k) plan is not a qualified plan.
    C. A 401(k) plan allows loans, and a 403(b) plan does not allow loans.
    D. A 501(c)(3) organization may establish a 403(b) plan but cannot establish a 401(k) plan.

71. A retirement plan is _____ if more than 60% of total plan benefits are in favor of key employees.

    A. ERISA certified
    B. discriminatory
    C. illegal
    D. top heavy

72. Which of the following entities will protect owners from liability beyond the amount they personally invested?

    (1) C Corp
    (2) Limited partnership
    (3) LLC
    (4) S Corp

    A. (1) and (4) only
    B. (2) and (3) only
    C. (1), (2), and (3) only
    D. (1), (3), and (4) only

73. Which of the following is a free tool from FINRA that is intended to help consumers research the professional backgrounds of brokers and brokerage firms, as well as investment adviser firms and advisers?

    A. BrokerCheck
    B. FirmCheck
    C. InvestorCheck
    D. None of the above are correct.

74. All but which of the following are characteristics of an LLC?

    A. It provides limited liability to all members.
    B. It dissolves upon the death, retirement, or resignation of a member unless the remaining members elect by majority to continue.
    C. An operating agreement is not required.
    D. Majority approval is required to transfer management or management rights.

For questions 75 – 77, match the form of the efficient market hypothesis with the description that follows. Use only one answer per blank. Answers may be used more than once or not at all.

A. Strong form
B. Semi-strong form
C. Weak form

75. ___ Historical price data is already reflected in the current stock price and there is no value in predicting future price changes. However, fundamental analysis may generate superior performance. Technical analysis will not produce superior results.

76. ___ All historical information and industry conditions are already reflected in stock prices. Neither technical nor fundamental analysis can produce superior results over time on a risk-adjusted basis. Possessing insider information may lead to achieving returns in excess of the market.

77. ___ All public and private information is already reflected in stock prices. Neither technical nor fundamental analysis can improve the efficiency of the market to determine prices. Possessing insider information is not a factor in outperforming the overall market.

78. Which of the following is the tangent line to the efficient frontier that passes through the risk-free rate on the expected return axis?

A. Capital market line
B. Security market line
C. Support line
D. Trendline

79. If $1 is deposited each year in an interest-bearing account earning 8.5% annually, and the interest is not withdrawn, the account value at the end of 3 years will be:

A. $3.12.
B. $3.18.
C. $3.26.
D. $3.44.

80. Puts are an option to _____ a specified number of shares of stock during a specified period at a specified price. A buyer of a put option expects the price of the underlying stock to _____.

A. buy, fall
B. buy, rise
C. sell, fall
D. sell, rise

81. Which of the following is an electronic quotation listing of the bid and asked prices of OTC stocks that do not meet the requirements to be listed on the NASDAQ stock-listing system?

A. ECN
B. Instinet
C. OTC Bulletin Board
D. OTC Quotation System

82. Which of the following is a tax imposed in such a manner that the tax rate increases as the amount subject to taxation decreases?

A. Flat tax
B. Progressive tax
C. Regressive tax
D. Value added tax

83. According to FINRA Rule 2210, "correspondence" is defined as any written (including electronic) communication that is distributed or made available to _____ or fewer retail investors within any _____ calendar-day period.

A. 25, 30
B. 25, 60
C. 50, 30
D. 50, 60

84. Carrie believes the share price of Zeta stock will decrease in the short term. She has decided to sell short 500 shares at the current market price of $89. If the initial margin requirement is 35%, what amount must Carrie contribute as margin?

A. $15,575
B. $17,250
C. $19,925
D. $21,485

85. Which of the following is correct regarding convertible bonds?

A. They typically offer lower coupon rates than non-convertible bonds issued for the same term by the same issuer.
B. They typically offer higher coupon rates than non-convertible bonds issued for the same term by the same issuer.
C. They typically offer the same coupon rates as non-convertible bonds issued for the same term by the same issuer.
D. They are zero-coupon bonds issued at a discount to par.

86. Form ADV is filed electronically through which of the following systems?

    A. BrokerCheck
    B. CRD
    C. IARD
    D. Instinet

87. Which of the following are necessary parties to a trust?

    A. Executor, decedent, beneficiary
    B. Trustee, beneficiary, administrator
    C. Trustor, trustee, beneficiary
    D. Trustor, decedent, administrator

88. Which of the following is correct regarding the SEC's guidance on the "testimonial rule" and social media?

    A. Testimonials were originally addressed in Rule 206(4)-1(a)(1) of the Investment Advisers Act of 1940.
    B. Advisers are allowed to select favorable testimonials to include on their websites only if client names are kept confidential.
    C. Advisers are allowed to select favorable testimonials to include on their websites only if they receive permission from the clients, and they post each client's full name.
    D. None of the above are correct.

For questions 89 – 91, match the cost recovery term with the description that follows. Use only one answer per blank. Answers may be used more than once or not at all.

    A. Amortization
    B. Depreciation
    C. Depletion

89. ___ The process by which the tax basis of natural resources is recovered.

90. ___ The process by which the tax basis of intangible assets is recovered.

91. ___ The process by which the tax basis of tangible assets is recovered.

92. Seth owns a 12-year-old property that is worth $339,500. If the property has depreciated at a rate of 2.5% per year, what was its original value?

    A. $480,000
    B. $485,000
    C. $490,000
    D. $495,000

93. An option that can be exercised at any time up to and including its expiration date is a/an _____ style option.

    A. American
    B. Asian
    C. Australian
    D. European

94. Which of the following forms is the "Uniform Application for Securities Industry Registration or Transfer," which representatives of broker-dealers, investment advisers, or issuers of securities must fill out in order to become registered in the appropriate jurisdictions?

    A. Form U4
    B. Form U5
    C. Form U6
    D. Form U7

95. Craig recently adopted a profit sharing plan for his business and he's unsure about the contribution rules. He'd like to know if he, as the employer, can contribute more than 25% to an employee's account in 2018. Which of the following should Craig be advised?

    A. Yes, the limit is the lesser of 100% or $55,000.
    B. No, the limit is 25%.
    C. Yes, but the total company contributions cannot exceed 25% of total plan compensation.
    D. Both A and C are correct.

96. Which of the following allows a firm to file one registration statement covering several issues of the same security? The securities can then be sold over a period of several years.

    A. Deferred registration
    B. Omitting registration
    C. Shelf registration
    D. Statutory registration

97. All qualified retirement plans must satisfy the reporting and disclosure requirements as specified by _____.

    A. ERISA
    B. the IRS
    C. the PBGC
    D. the SEC

98. If an insured borrows a portion of the cash value from her whole life insurance policy, which of the following is true?

(1) The loan can be for an amount up to 100% of the face value of the policy.
(2) The loan must be repaid within five years.
(3) The loan will not charge interest.
(4) Any outstanding loans must be deducted from the face amount of the policy before death benefits are paid.

A. (4) only
B. (1) and (2) only
C. (1), (2), and (4) only
D. All of the above are correct.

99. Which of the following is a type of preferred stock that gives the investor the right to receive dividends equal to the normally specified rate, as well as an additional dividend based on a specific predetermined condition?

A. Accumulating preferred stock
B. Dividend preferred stock
C. Non-participating preferred stock
D. Participating preferred stock

100. A diversified mutual fund cannot own more than _____ of the shares of a given company or more than _____ of fund assets in a given investment.

A. 5%, 5%
B. 10%, 5%
C. 20%, 10%
D. 20%, 20%

101. Which of the following refers to the trading of exchange-listed securities in the over-the-counter market? These trades allow institutional investors to trade blocks of securities directly, rather than through an exchange, providing liquidity and anonymity to buyers.

A. First market
B. Second market
C. Third market
D. Fourth market

102. The Dow Jones Transportation Average is an index comprised of _____ transportation stocks.

A. 20
B. 30
C. 50
D. 100

The following information relates to questions 103 – 104.

Alpha Corporation is investing $900,000 in a new production facility. The present value of the future after-tax cash flows is estimated to be $950,000. Alpha Corporation currently has 80,000 outstanding shares of stock with a current market price of $14.00 per share.

103. What will be the value of Alpha Corporation after the investment?

    A. $1,120,000
    B. $1,170,000
    C. $1,190,000
    D. $1,204,000

104. The "conduit theory," which states that qualifying investment firms, such as REITs, should not be taxed like regular companies because interest, dividends, and capital gains are passed directly to shareholders who are then taxed on the income, is found in which of the following sections of the Internal Revenue Code?

    A. Subchapter J
    B. Subchapter K
    C. Subchapter M
    D. Subchapter S

105. All but which of the following are considered quantitative data?

    A. Cash flow statement
    B. Insurance coverage
    C. Investment portfolio
    D. Lifestyle and priorities

106. Which of the following may cause a will to be considered invalid?

    (1) The testator was influenced by another person.
    (2) The testator did not have adequate mental capacity to execute a will.

    A. (1) only
    B. (2) only
    C. Both (1) and (2) are correct.
    D. Neither (1) or (2) are correct.

107. If an individual contributes more to an IRA than is permitted, the excess contribution is subject to which of the following taxes?

    A. 5% excise tax
    B. 6% excise tax
    C. 10% excise tax
    D. 15% excise tax

The following information relates to questions 108 – 110.

An analyst provides the following information for Epsilon Corporation's fiscal year:

Revenue	$550,000
Cost of sales	$325,000
Gross profit	$225,000
Marketing costs	$55,000
Operating income	$170,000
Interest and other expenses, net	$20,000
Earnings before taxes	$150,000

108. What is Epsilon Corporation's gross profit margin?

   A. 27.3%
   B. 33.4%
   C. 40.9%
   D. 63.7%

109. What is Epsilon Corporation's operating profit margin?

   A. 27.3%
   B. 30.9%
   C. 51.2%
   D. 75.6%

110. What is Epsilon Corporation's pretax margin?

   A. 27.3%
   B. 40.9%
   C. 53.5%
   D. 66.7%

111. What will be the value of Alpha Corporation's share price after the investment?

   A. $14.63
   B. $15.26
   C. $15.89
   D. $16.12

112. Which of the following is a formal contract between a bond issuer and a bondholder?

   A. Debenture agreement
   B. Indenture agreement
   C. Prospectus agreement
   D. Tombstone agreement

113. Which of the following imposed an obligation on the SEC to consider the impacts that any new regulation would have on competition, and empowered the SEC to establish a national market system and a system for nationwide clearing and settlement of securities transactions?

    A. Uniform Securities Act of 1956
    B. Securities Act Amendments of 1975
    C. Uniform Prudent Investors Act of 1994
    D. National Securities Market Improvement Act of 1996

114. All but which of the following are characteristics of REITs?

    A. Losses cannot be passed through to investors to deduct personally.
    B. REIT shareholders are subject to double taxation.
    C. REITs can be purchased in small denominations.
    D. All of the above are correct.

115. Which of the following will typically require an RIA firm to register or notice file in a state?

    A. The RIA firm has a physical presence in the state.
    B. The RIA firm has more than 5 clients who are located in the state.
    C. The RIA firm is actively soliciting in the state.
    D. All of the above are correct.

116. Which of the following are prohibited investments in an IRA?

    (1) U.S. minted gold coins
    (2) Antiques
    (3) U.S. stamps
    (4) Art work

    A. (1) only
    B. (1), (2), and (4) only
    C. (2), (3), and (4) only
    D. All of the above are correct.

117. All but which of the following are correct regarding the correlation coefficient?

    A. Two securities that have a correlation coefficient of $+1$ are perfectly positively correlated. The two securities will move in the exact same direction.
    B. Two securities that have a correlation coefficient of -1 are perfectly negatively correlated. The two securities will move exactly opposite each other.
    C. If two securities have a correlation coefficient of zero, there is no correlation between the price changes of the two securities.
    D. Risk is eliminated when the correlation coefficient between two securities is zero because the portfolio standard deviation will also be zero.

118. Which of the following is the rate of return that causes the net present value of all cash flows received from an investment to equal zero?

    A. CAPM
    B. IRR
    C. NPV
    D. TEY

119. Which of the following SEC regulations requires firms to have policies and procedures addressing the protection of customer information and records? This regulation also requires firms to provide initial and annual privacy notices to customers describing information sharing policies.

    A. Regulation FD
    B. Regulation MA-W
    C. Regulation N-Q
    D. Regulation S-P

120. All but which of the following are correct regarding a futures contract?

    A. It is an agreement to buy or sell a specific quantity of a commodity or financial currency at a predetermined price on a specific future date.
    B. The holder of a futures contract cannot purchase an offsetting contract that cancels the original position, rather than receiving delivery of the commodity.
    C. Commodities such as grains, metals, and natural gas do not have tradable futures contracts.
    D. All of the above are correct.

For questions 121 – 128, match the type of retirement plan with the description that follows. Use only one answer per blank. Answers may be used more than once or not at all.

    A. Profit sharing plan
    B. Pension plan

121. ___ 401(k) plan

122. ___ Money purchase plan

123. ___ Stock bonus plan

124. ___ ESOP

125. ___ Target benefit plan

126. ___ Thrift savings plan

127. ___ Cash balance plan

128. ___ SEP

129. Last year, an investor allocated her portfolio in the following asset classes:

Asset Class	Asset Allocation (%)	Asset Class Return (%)
Domestic equities	40.0	+10.0
International equities	20.0	−4.0
Corporate bonds	30.0	+6.0
Money market funds	10.0	+2.0

What was the portfolio's weighted average return for the year?

A. 4.8%
B. 5.2%
C. 5.6%
D. 5.8%

130. Alex, age 70, has contributed $20,000 to a Roth IRA throughout his career. The account value is now $30,000. If Alex withdraws the entire amount, how much tax will he owe if he's in the 28% tax bracket?

A. $0
B. $1,500
C. $4,500
D. $8,400

ANSWER KEY

1. D
All employees, age 21 or older, who performed services during the current year and earned at least $600 in three out of the past five years, must be eligible to participate in a SEP. Employer contributions to a SEP are not subject to FICA/FUTA withholding. A SEP does not need to provide for a qualified preretirement survivor annuity (QPSA), and loans from a SEP are not permitted.

2. A
Because they are growing and expanding, growth stocks typically do not pay large dividends. Most of the earnings generated from growth stocks are reinvested back into the company.

3. C
HPR = [($6,000 + $400) – $5,500] ÷ $5,500 = 0.1636 = 16.36%

4. D
Underwriting refers to the process of selecting, classifying, and pricing applicants for insurance. The underwriter is the individual who decides to accept or reject an application, and under what conditions the policy may be issued. One of the objectives of underwriting is to generate revenue while at the same time limiting the insurance company's assumed risk. Restrictive underwriting typically results in lower overall claims made by policyholders.

5. A
According to modern portfolio theory, a client's optimal portfolio is located at the point of tangency of the investor's indifference curve and the efficient frontier of available investment assets.

6. B
($4,000 × 0.28) – $1,000 = $120
The deduction is more beneficial because it creates the equivalent of a $1,120 credit, which is $120 more than the $1,000 credit.

7. A
Rights of accumulation allow investors to aggregate their own holdings as well as the holdings of certain related parties, such as spouses and children, toward achieving the investment thresholds at which breakpoint discounts become available.

8. B
A currency transaction report (CTR) must be filed by U.S. financial institutions for each deposit, withdrawal, exchange of currency, or other payment to the institution which involves a transaction in currency of more than $10,000.

9. C
A simple trust is required to pay out all of its income annually to trust beneficiaries and cannot distribute trust principal. A complex trust may accumulate income or make distributions from trust principal.

10. A
Purchasing power risk is a type of systematic risk.

11. B
Business risk is a type of unsystematic risk.

12. A
Market risk is a type of systematic risk.

13. B
Financial risk is a type of unsystematic risk.

14. A
Interest rate risk is a type of systematic risk.

15. A
Exchange rate risk is a type of systematic risk.

16. B
The maximum criminal fine for an individual who commits an insider trading violation is $5 million.

17. B
$S^n = (1 + i)^n$
$S^n = (1.085)^3 = \$1.28$

18. B
Buying a call and selling a put are both bullish strategies.

19. C
According to the Uniform Securities Act, warrants are classified as securities. Collectibles, fixed annuities, and whole life insurance policies are not classified as securities.

20. D
The PPI (Producer Price Index) is a weighted index of prices measured at the wholesale level.

21. C
Distributions from a 401(k) plan following separation from service after age 55 are not subject to the 10% premature distribution penalty.

22. B
Defined benefit plans favor older employees, and actuarial calculations are required. The employer assumes the investment risk in a defined benefit plan.

23. D
Negotiable CDs are short-term, fixed-income securities that may be bought or sold in the open market at a market-determined price.

24. A
Debt-to-capital ratio = Total debt ÷ (Total debt + Shareholders' equity)
Debt-to-capital ratio = $44,100 ÷ ($44,100 + $57,500) = 0.434 = 43.4%

25. C
ERISA Section 404(c) offers a safe harbor for retirement plan fiduciaries to not be liable for investment losses suffered by plan participants who self-direct their investments.

26. A
Viatical payments to a terminally ill insured are non-taxable if he or she has a life expectancy of two years or less.

27. A
The U.S. government conducts fiscal policy through government spending and taxation.

28. D
A health savings account (HSA) can be used to pay for the account owner's deductibles, copayments, and coinsurance.

29. C
TIPS (Treasury inflation-protected securities) are indexed to the rate of inflation as measured by the CPI.

30. D
ADV Part 1 typically includes affiliations, company ownership, and disciplinary history. It does not include a fee schedule.

31. A
Insurance company regulation occurs primarily at the state level. Broker-dealers are regulated at the federal level.

32. A
For Treasury STRIPS, tax must be paid on accrued interest each year even though no interest is received by the investor.

33. B
Prices for goods and services will inflate when their demand exceeds their supply.

34. A
A 403(b) plan may be adopted by an employer that is a state, agency of a state, nonprofit organization, public university, or private university.

35. D
The three main types of REITs are equity REITs, mortgage REITs, and hybrid REITs.

36. D
A "penny stock" is an equity security that trades below $5.

37. C
$5 \times \$15,000 = \$75,000$
A donor may contribute a total of five gift tax annual exclusion amounts on a one-time basis every five years to a 529 plan.

38. A
A defined benefit plan favors older owner/employees and would provide the greatest retirement benefit to Pete.

39. A
Open-end mutual funds sell at their net asset value (NAV) and do not have a fixed capital structure.

40. B
According to Rule 206(4)-5 adopted by the SEC under the Investment Advisers Act of 1940, investment advisers are prohibited from providing advisory services for compensation to a government entity client for 2 years after the adviser has made a contribution to certain elected officials or candidates.

41. C
A transferor's spouse or former spouse, regardless of age, is not a skip person for GSTT purposes. A grandchild of a transferor is not a skip person if the transferor's child is deceased at the time of transfer.

42. C
Money market funds can be redeemed at any time without penalty. Their objective is to earn interest for shareholders.

43. E
A certificate of deposit is intended to be held until maturity, but can be redeemed prior to maturity for a penalty.

44. D
Commercial paper is an unsecured promissory note issued by a corporation with a fixed maturity of up to 270 days.

45. B
Treasury bonds pay a fixed rate of interest every six months until maturity. They are issued in terms of ten years or more.

46. F
American Depository Receipt dividends are declared in local currencies and paid in U.S. dollars.

47. B
A red herring is the first prospectus released for a new issue and is intended to solicit indications of interest. It does not contain the new issue's price, and it is subject to change.

48. D
The 25% penalty for early withdrawals does not apply to SIMPLE 401(k) plans. It only applies to SIMPLE IRAs. For a SIMPLE 401(k) plan, the early withdrawal penalty is always 10%.

49. B
Duration is a measure of the timing of cash flows (i.e., the interest payments and the principal repayment) to be received from a fixed income security. It's used to assess price volatility for changes in interest rates and the reinvestment risk associated with a portfolio.

50. B
If corporate bonds are selling at a significant premium, then newly issued bonds are selling with lower coupons. The corporations are likely to call their bonds and replace them with lower coupon bonds.

51. A
If an investor's brokerage firm goes out of business and is a member of the SIPC, then the investor's cash and securities held by the firm may be protected up to $500,000, including a $250,000 limit for cash.

52. C
A flat yield curve generally indicates an economic slowdown. It occurs when there is little difference between short-term and long-term yields for debt instruments of the same credit quality.

53. B
Interest rate risk is the risk that, as interest rates rise, bond prices will fall. Interest rate risk is measured by a bond's duration.

54. C
The maximum criminal fine for a non-natural person (such as an entity whose securities are publicly traded) who commits an insider trading violation is $25 million.

55. C
Regulation U sets out certain requirements for lenders, other than securities brokers and dealers, who extend credit secured by margin stock.

56. D
According to the anomaly known as the P/E effect, low P/E stocks appear to outperform high P/E stocks over annual periods after being adjusted for risk and size.

57. B
An actuary calculates the required amount of an employer's annual contribution to a defined benefit plan to ensure that current and future plan benefits are available to the participants.

58. B
The liquidity ratios are the current ratio and quick ratio.

59. B

The Securities Exchange Act of 1934 created the SEC and empowered it with broad authority over all aspects of the securities industry.

60. C

Earnings before interest and taxes (EBIT) ÷ Annual sales = Operating profit margin

61. A

When a person dies leaving a will, he or she is said to die testate. When a person dies without leaving a will, he or she dies intestate.

62. D

A bond swap can potentially reduce an investor's tax liability, provide a higher rate of return, and provide investment diversification.

63. C

If a corporation is required to pay unpaid dividends from prior years before paying a dividend to common stockholders, the stock is considered to be cumulative preferred stock.

64. A

To be considered an accredited investor, earned income must exceed $200,000 (or $300,000 together with a spouse) in each of the prior two years, and must be reasonably expected to occur for the current year.

65. B

Sharpe ratio = $(R_p - R_f) \div S_p$

Sharpe ratio = $(0.15 - 0.04) \div 0.07 = 1.57$

66. B

Profit sharing plans tend to favor younger employees, and they are not limited in their investment of company stock. Profit sharing plans are a type of defined contribution plan other than a pension plan. Their contributions must be substantial and recurring, but are not required annually.

67. B

The Patriot Act of 2001 provides the tools required to intercept and obstruct terrorism. Title III of this act is intended to facilitate the prevention, detection, and prosecution of international money laundering and the financing of terrorism.

68. D

Unless the house was bought by Lynn with money earned prior to marriage, or with gift or inheritance money, the house is community property. The question does not provide this information, and it cannot be assumed. Therefore, Lynn's half of the house will pass by will. Tom already owns half of the house under community property laws.

69. B

The family limited partnership and QPRT (qualified personal residence trust) can potentially reduce Nicholas's gross estate. The living trust and Totten trust will reduce the probate estate, but not the gross estate.

70. A
A 401(k) plan is a qualified plan, and a 403(b) plan is not a qualified plan.

71. D
A retirement plan is top heavy if more than 60% of total plan benefits are in favor of key employees. Certain rules and conditions apply to top-heavy plans.

72. D
The LLC, C Corp, and S Corp will protect investors from liability beyond the amount they personally invested. In a limited partnership, the general partner has unlimited liability.

73. A
BrokerCheck is a free tool from FINRA that is intended to help consumers research the professional backgrounds of brokers and brokerage firms, as well as investment adviser firms and advisers.

74. C
An LLC provides limited liability to all members, and it dissolves upon the death, retirement, or resignation of a member unless the remaining members elect by majority to continue. Majority approval is required to transfer management or management rights, and an operating agreement is required to determine the management structure of an LLC.

75. C
According to the weak form of the efficient market hypothesis, historical price data is already reflected in the current stock price and there is no value in predicting future price changes. However, fundamental analysis may generate superior performance. Technical analysis will not produce superior results.

76. B
According to the semi-strong form of the efficient market hypothesis, all historical information and industry conditions are already reflected in stock prices. Neither technical nor fundamental analysis can produce superior results over time on a risk-adjusted basis. Possessing insider information may lead to achieving returns in excess of the market.

77. A
According to the strong form of the efficient market hypothesis, all public and private information is already reflected in stock prices. Neither technical nor fundamental analysis can improve the efficiency of the market to determine prices. Possessing insider information is not a factor in outperforming the overall market.

78. A
The capital market line is the tangent line to the efficient frontier that passes through the risk-free rate on the expected return axis.

79. C
$S_n = [(1 + i)^n - 1] \div i$
$S_n = [(1.085)^3 - 1] \div 0.085 = \$3.26$

80. C
Puts are an option to sell a specified number of shares of stock during a specified period at a specified price. A buyer of a put option expects the price of the underlying stock to fall.

81. C
The OTC Bulletin Board is an electronic quotation listing of the bid and asked prices of OTC stocks that do not meet the requirements to be listed on the NASDAQ stock-listing system.

82. B
A progressive tax is imposed in such a manner that the tax rate increases as the amount subject to taxation decreases.

83. A
According to FINRA Rule 2210, "correspondence" is defined as any written (including electronic) communication that is distributed or made available to 25 or fewer retail investors within any 30 calendar-day period.

84. A
500 shares × $89 per share × 0.35 = $15,575

85. A
Because of their flexibility, convertible bonds typically offer lower coupon rates than non-convertible bonds issued for the same term by the same issuer.

86. C
Form ADV is filed electronically through the IARD (Investment Adviser Registration Depository).

87. C
The necessary parties to a trust are the trustor, trustee, and beneficiary.

88. A
Testimonials were originally addressed in Rule 206(4)-1(a)(1) of the Investment Advisers Act of 1940. In general, client testimonials are not permitted to be included on adviser websites and social media.

89. C
Depletion is the process by which the tax basis of natural resources is recovered.

90. A
Amortization is the process by which the tax basis of intangible assets is recovered.

91. B
Depreciation is the process by which the tax basis of tangible assets is recovered.

92. B
Step 1: Accumulated depreciation = 12 years × 0.025 per year = 0.3
Step 2: Original value = $339,500 ÷ (1 – 0.3) = $485,000

93. A

An option that can be exercised at any time up to and including its expiration date is an American style option.

94. A

Form U4 is the "Uniform Application for Securities Industry Registration or Transfer," which representatives of broker-dealers, investment advisers, or issuers of securities must fill out in order to become registered in the appropriate jurisdictions.

95. D

Craig can contribute more than 25% to an individual employee's account, but the contributions must remain under the IRC Section 415 limit. The total company contributions cannot exceed 25% of total plan compensation.

96. C

Shelf registrations allows a firm to file one registration statement covering several issues of the same security. The securities can then be sold over a period of several years.

97. A

All qualified retirement plans must satisfy the reporting and disclosure requirements as specified by ERISA.

98. A

Any outstanding policy loans must be deducted from the face amount of a life insurance policy before death benefits are paid. Insureds can typically borrow an amount up to the cash value of the policy, not the face value.

99. D

Participating preferred stock gives the investor the right to receive dividends equal to the normally specified rate, as well as an additional dividend based on a specific predetermined condition.

100. B

A diversified mutual fund cannot own more than 10% of the shares of a given company or more than 5% of fund assets in a given investment.

101. C

Third market refers to the trading of exchange-listed securities in the over-the-counter market. These trades allow institutional investors to trade blocks of securities directly, rather than through an exchange, providing liquidity and anonymity to buyers.

102. A

The Dow Jones Transportation Average is an index comprised of 20 transportation stocks.

103. B

($14.00 per share × 80,000 shares) + ($950,000 – $900,000) = $1,170,000

104. C
The "conduit theory," which states that qualifying investment firms, such as REITs, should not be taxed like regular companies because interest, dividends, and capital gains are passed directly to shareholders who are then taxed on the income, is found in Subchapter M of the Internal Revenue Code.

105. D
Insurance coverage, a cash flow statement, and an investment portfolio are considered quantitative data. Lifestyle and priorities are qualitative data.

106. B
A will may be considered invalid if the testator did not act of his or her own free will, or if the testator did not have adequate mental capacity to execute a will. Simply being influenced by another person does not cause a will to be considered invalid.

107. B
If an individual contributes more to an IRA than is permitted, the excess contribution is subject to a 6% excise tax.

108. C
Gross profit margin = Gross profit ÷ Revenue
Gross profit margin = $225,000 ÷ $550,000 = 0.409 = 40.9%

109. B
Operating profit margin = Operating income ÷ Revenue
Operating profit margin = $170,000 ÷ $550,000 = 0.309 = 30.9%

110. A
Pretax margin = Earnings before taxes ÷ Revenue
Pretax margin = $150,000 ÷ $550,000 = 0.273 = 27.3%

111. A
Step 1: ($950,000 – $900,000) ÷ 80,000 shares = $0.63
Step 2: $14.00 + $0.63 = $14.63

112. B
An indenture agreement is a formal contract between a bond issuer and a bondholder.

113. B
The Securities Act Amendments of 1975 imposed an obligation on the SEC to consider the impacts that any new regulation would have on competition, and empowered the SEC to establish a national market system and a system for nationwide clearing and settlement of securities transactions.

114. B
REITs can be purchased in small denominations, and losses cannot be passed through to investors to deduct personally. REIT shareholders are not subject to double taxation.

115. D

An RIA firm will be required to register or notice file in a state if the RIA firm has a physical presence in the state, or if it has more than 5 clients who are located in the state, or if the firm is actively soliciting in the state.

116. C

Collectibles that are prohibited investments in IRAs include antiques, stamps, art work, rugs, metals, gems, stamps, and coins. There is an exception for U.S. minted gold coins.

117. D

Risk is eliminated when the correlation coefficient between two securities is −1. If two securities have a correlation coefficient of zero, there is no correlation between the price changes of the two securities.

118. B

The internal rate of return (IRR) is the rate of return that causes the net present value of all cash flows received from an investment to equal zero.

119. D

Regulation S-P requires firms to have policies and procedures addressing the protection of customer information and records. This regulation also requires firms to provide initial and annual privacy notices to customers describing information sharing policies.

120. B

A futures contract is an agreement to buy or sell a specific quantity of a commodity or financial currency at a predetermined price on a specific future date. The holder of a futures contract may purchase an offsetting contract that cancels the original position, rather than receiving delivery of the commodity. Commodities such as grains, metals, and natural gas all have tradable futures contracts.

121. A

A 401(k) plan is a type of profit sharing plan.

122. B

A money purchase plan is a type of pension plan.

123. A

A stock bonus plan is a type of profit sharing plan.

124. A

An ESOP is a type of profit sharing plan.

125. B

A target benefit plan is a type of pension plan.

126. A

A thrift savings plan is a type of profit sharing plan.

127. B

A cash balance plan is a type of pension plan.

128. B
A SEP is a type of pension plan.

129. B
$R_p = w_1R_1 + w_2R_2 + w_3R_3 + w_4R_4$
$R_p = (0.40 \times 0.10) + (0.20 \times -0.04) + (0.30 \times 0.06) + (0.10 \times 0.02)$
$R_p = 0.04 - 0.008 + 0.018 + 0.002 = 0.052 = 5.2\%$

130. A
Roth IRA contributions are made with after-tax dollars and grow tax-free. Alex will not owe taxes when he takes the distribution.

INDEX

Index

U

V

W – Z

CPSIA information can be obtained
at www.ICGtesting.com
Printed in the USA
LVHW040824240322
714086LV00005B/570

9 781732 113756